Memories from a Misty Morning Marsh

...a duck hunter's collection

Text & Photos by Larry Dablemont

Illustrations by Tom Goldsmith

Lightnin' Ridge Books

Box 22
Bolivar • MO 65613

Memories of a Misty Morning Marsh
A duck hunter's collection

Copyright 1999 by Larry Dablemont

Published by
Lightning Ridge Books

Illustrations
Tom Goldsmith

Photography
Larry Dablemont

Editing and designing
Randy Jones

ISBN: 0-9673975-1-0

LIBRARY OF CONGRESS CATALOG NUMBER: 99-96996

Table of Contents...

Chapter 1 - A DUCK HUNTER IS. 1

Chapter 2 - THE FIRST HUNT 5

Chapter 3 - THE BEST THERE EVER WAS 15

Chapter 4 - A GOOD SPREAD OF DECOYS 27

Chapter 5 - ALADDIN'S STORY 39

Chapter 6 - A GOOD SET OF WADERS. 53

Chapter 7 - A DAY IN OL' F-13. 61

Chapter 8 - A LITTLE HISTORY. 69

Chapter 9 - SHOOTING STEEL. 75

Chapter 10 - AS THE WIND BLOWS 85

Chapter 11 - HUNTING WITH A JONAH 99

Chapter 12 - DUCKS IN THE GOOD OL' DAYS. 109

Chapter 13 - A FAMILY OF MALLARDS 119

Chapter 14 - PUDDLE DUCKS 127

Chapter. 15 - WOOD DUCKS 135

Chapter 16 - TRASH DUCKS. 145

Chapter 17 - BORN OF BLIZZARDS 155

Chapter 18 - MANITOBA GEESE. 163

Chapter 19 - SWEATING AND SWATTING 179

Chapter 20 - LETTERS FROM A DUCK HUNTER. . . . 189

Chapter 21 - GRONK AND THE BEGINNINGS 199

Chapter 22 - POETRY FOR THE DUCK HUNTER . . . 205

A Word from the Author

There have been a great number of books written about duck hunting just to make you a better duck hunter. This one probably won't help you much unless you are a real beginner. Let's face it, if you are an expert duck hunter, [and most of us are] you can't learn much, you already know it. All us experts ever really do is sit around and argue about how many decoys to use, what makes the best loads, whose Labrador is best and whose face is flaring the ducks.

If you get a South Dakota duck hunter together with an East Arkansas duck hunter, you can really have an argument, because neither of the two know much about how the other one hunts. Hunting ducks in green timber is a different sport than hunting ducks in the Missouri river bottoms. Hunting ducks in the sandhill lakes of Nebraska isn't anything like hunting ducks on small waters among the cornfields in Iowa, and hunting ducks in the Delta Marsh country of Manitoba and Saskatchewan is something different than either of other two places.

The hunters on Lake of the Woods in Ontario who head out to hunt bluebills when the first bad weather hits in late October don't care much how we hunt mallards in waders in the back of a Truman Lake cove, and the fellows who build a permanent blind in an Illinois duck club don't understand a thing about using a boat blind way up the Arkansas River. So how are you going to write a book to make them all better duck hunters? Not me. I just wanted to write a book for outdoorsmen who love to hunt ducks.

I hope you learn something, but most of all, I hope this book causes you to hear the wind off the wings as mallards pass overhead, and feel the sleet as it bounces off your face, and smell the burned gunpowder and the wet Labradors. I hope it causes you to nod your head and say, "Yeah, I've seen the same thing," or chuckle beneath your breath and say, "I hunted with a guy like that," or even laugh out loud and say, "Boy, I've had that same thing happen to me!" I hope you have some laughs, get nostalgic and recall some of the good ol' days from your own past hunts.

It's those memories from a misty morning marsh that makes duck hunting a real obsession. If you aren't there yet, maybe this book will hclp you along.

i

Dave Meisner, 1945-1998

Dedication

This book is dedicated to the memory of Dave Meisner, a good friend and hunting companion, who died in December of 1998 at the age of 53 from a sudden stroke. He was the publisher of The Retriever Journal, and had founded and published Gun Dog Magazine in 1980 before selling it in 1985. Some of the chapters in this book were published in those two magazines, and it was Dave who first urged me to write a book such as this one. He loved dogs, he loved to hunt, and he loved people. There was always a smile on his face, regardless of the substantial personal problems he sometimes faced. Because of that outgoing personality and a wonderful sense of humor, no one who hunted with him will ever forget him. He put God first in his life, and it showed.

I doubt that I will ever begin a duck season on a lonely marsh without thinking of Dave, without seeing him there in my mind. And I will never forget that few things are more important in all this world than close friends, and nothing creates closer friendships than days spent on a misty morning marsh, where the glory of God's greatest creation surrounds us. It was something Dave Meisner knew as well.

Chapter 1

A Duck Hunter Is...

He is the picture of optimism on opening day, when dawn brings first light to the marsh. He watches the skies in nervous anticipation of the first flock, and begs a high-flying single to look closer at the decoys.

To a non-hunter, he seems a strange sort, out there in the mud and the cold and the dampness, but the duck hunter never asks for anyone's approval. He is an independent sort, who likes nothing better than the most remote wetlands, cold gray skies and just enough wind to keep the decoys moving.

A duck hunter is a man who finds value in a pair of patched waders that should have been replaced years ago, a wooden decoy with the paint worn off and a Labrador pup that might make a retriever... someday. His treasures are old duck calls and duck bands, and pump shotguns that look like they've been through a war.

He is a man who gets fidgety in the first 30 minutes of a shopping trip with his wife, but he can sit for 10 hours in a cramped duck blind and never complain.

He's the same fellow that drives to work at 7:00 a.m. droopy-eyed and yawning, but at 4:00 a.m. on opening day, he's as bright-eyed as a first grader on Christmas morning.

He likes everyone during duck season. His only enemy is the guy who sets a raft of decoys 70 yards away and blows a duck call like he's at a New Year's Eve party.

A duck hunter often thinks his buddies' best call sounds like a hen mallard with a sore throat, while his own call sounds even better than that calling tape he ordered. But he is tolerant of his friends. On occasion, with his limit in hand, he might offer to shoot one or two for a hunting partner!

He is also tolerant of ice as long as it's thin enough to break, and the cold as long as it doesn't cause his old automatic to jam. He is not so tolerant of bluebird days, coots and people who fish during duck season.

Most any duck hunter likes coffee that stays hot in a thermos bottle, blizzards one hundred miles to the north, and early mallards.

He looks forward to the bowl games, 'cause they thin out the competition and he can hunt his favorite places alone.

He doesn't complain much in October and November, but he's hard to live with in late January.

He's an adventurer, up against adversity such as intense cold, mud that sucks at the waders, and water that gets deep in a hurry. Underwater stumps and submerged limbs and logs sometimes provide more adventure than he needs. A duck hunter knows all about building a fire in a hurry, and trying to dry clothes over an open flame.

He has endured a little of everything for his sport, including the outlay of great sums of money. In fact, his money has been the salvation of waterfowl. He has financed wetland preservation, funded refuges and bolstered habitat for all wild things in the process.

He has led the fight for competent waterfowl management, and for bag limits and game laws that are designed to ensure that there will be new hunters to fill his hip-boots in distant December marshes.

The best friend of waterfowl is this man, the duck hunter. At the end of a season, the ducks in the freezer may not dent the grocery bill much, but memories of days in the blind are priceless treasures.

Green-wings streaking over the decoys like a squadron of tiny jet fighters, or red-legged mallards dropping in like leaves from a fall breeze never cease to touch his very soul, no matter how often he has experienced those things.

When the evening sun sets at the edge of the marsh, the decoys are bagged and guns emptied, and the duck

hunter heads for solid footing... the concrete and pavement of everyday life, he does so with the knowledge that days spent in a duck blind make civilization at least more bearable, if not rational.

At the end of such a day, he will pause for a final moment in the last light of a dying sunset to watch a string of geese pass against the orange sky. And lifting his collar against the fall chill, he always wonders.... what would it be like to join them?

My grandfather poses with ducks from the Big Piney river in 1927.

Chapter 2

The First Hunt

I went on my first duck hunt a week or so after my eleventh birthday. It was a memorable hunt alright…that was the day my dad fell out of a tree and broke three ribs.

I would almost bet that no matter how many books you read on duck-hunting, you'll never read another one by an author who's dad fell out of a tree on his first duck hunt. Well it's a long story so I'll start at the beginning.

And it actually began when my grandfather moved to the Big Piney River as a small boy just after the turn of the century. His family moved to a farm on the lower part of the river near Edgar Springs, Missouri. Grandpa and his brother Perry were fascinated by the clean, clear river and the abundance of wildlife along it. In that day, there were no big reservoirs in the lower Midwest, and families grew corn and other crops in the river bottoms. In the fall, thousands of migrating ducks settled in to eat acorns along the river and feed in the adjacent cornfields.

My grandfather 's first duck-hunting was done with a muzzle-loading shotgun, and he'd sneak up over river banks to flush unsuspecting mallards and wood ducks resting in the pockets. When he was a teenager, a rise in the river brought him a boat which had been carried from upstream. He dug it out of a drift when the river went down, a wooden boat built much like a feed trough. He used it long enough to begin to see ways to improve it, and just before World War I he traded some furs for rough-cut pine lumber from a local sawmill and made his own john-boat.

Returning from the war, he made more of them, and began to make money fishing and trapping the river. Then one fall, he got the idea of stacking boughs of maple, oak and willow on the front of his boat and sneaking up on ducks along the stream. Using the sassafras paddles he also made, my grandfather was unbelievably good at easing quietly along the river, floating to within a few yards of wildlife by concealing his boat and himself with that blind. And waterfowl was so numerous back then that at times flocks of 50 to 100 ducks were found in the eddies below the shoals.

Grandpa married my grandmother, who also lived on a river bottom farm several miles upstream, and he raised a daughter and four sons on the Big Piney, continuing to make his living trapping, selling fish, making and selling john-boats and eventually guiding fishermen who came from the city. When the fishing slowed in the winter, he took them duck-hunting behind his floating blind.

As his sons grew old enough, they too began to guide, and hunters came from all over the Midwest to float the river for ducks. It was much different than the decoy hunting the outdoor magazines spoke of, but it was exciting, spotting a flock of mallards two hundred yards down river and setting out to paddle right up into the midst of them.

My grandfather and his sons could do things with a wooden john-boat and a sassafras paddle that would amaze the hunters and fishermen who came to float the river with them. And when I was a small boy and dad and grandpa came in with limits of wild ducks taken from a day on the river, I was fascinated with them. I'd ask for all the details of the hunt as they picked and cleaned ducks, and I'd collect feathers from the drakes and beg to go with them.

During the fall of my eleventh birthday, dad agreed that I was old enough to go along. That November morning we pushed the old john-boat out into the shrouds of mist rising from the river with me sitting right behind the blind on the bow. I was shivering from the cold and the excitement. Finally, even though I didn't have a gun.... I was duck-hunting.

It was a cool,clear day with fallen leaves thick along

the river. I tried to see everything at once. In the McKinney eddy, there was a lone mallard swimming around in the middle of the river amongst the fallen leaves, and dad spotted him before he saw us. We eased closer and closer as I sat watching the mallard through the blind, shaking with buck fever. Then dad turned the boat and the mallard took to flight. His old '97 Winchester twelve-gauge roared and the duck folded. I picked it from the water and set it beside me to admire as we floated along. This one would probably join some others for Thanksgiving dinner at our house.

At the end of the eddy a fox squirrel scooted up a tree, and dad shot it too. It fell dead to the crotch of a limb coming off the main trunk about twelve or fifteen feet above the river bank, and hung there. Dad wasn't the kind of hunter to kill something and leave it, so he decided to climb up and get the squirrel. The tree had a little bit of lean to it, and there was a smaller tree next to it, so it shouldn't be all that hard to do even in hip boots.

He was almost to the squirrel when he lost his footing and came crashing down onto the tree roots sticking out of the bank, then bounced off them into the river. I was panic-stricken, but I grabbed his coat collar and pulled as hard as I could as my dad tried to crawl from the river up onto flat ground. I don't know if I helped much, but finally he was lying on his back in the leaves beneath the big tree with blood covering his face from a cut over his eye. Soaking wet, moaning and gasping for breath, he seemed in great pain, and I remember thinking dad was dying for sure. But he came around a little, and he told me there was a road about a mile away, and how to find it.

I remember praying as I ran through the woods and the fields, praying that God would help me find the road, and that He would keep my dad from dying there on the cold river bank before I could get back. And I remember flying over fences I might have struggled to cross on other days. Finally the road was there in front of me, and a man in an old Ford was driving along it, heading for town. He

7

had to stop, because I ran squarely into his path to stop him. He tried to calm me down, and then listened to my hysterical pleas for help. Luckily, he knew of an old road which descended to the river, not far from where dad was hurt, and he said he thought he could drive down it, but he wasn't sure if he could drive back up it.

Maybe the most anxiety I have ever felt developed as we descended that old road at what seemed like a snails pace. I wanted him to get there faster, certainly I had ran up those hills in less time than he was getting down them. And then we were there, and I was running toward where I had left my dad with the stranger yelling for me to slow down so he could keep up.

I just couldn't believe dad was still alive, but he was. He even managed to get to his feet with our help, and somehow we got to the car. Wet and bloody, dad was over six feet

Grandpa and my dad came back with these ducks from the Big Piney, well before I was born. Dad was 19 at the time, in November of 1946.

8

tall and about 200 pounds. I was only about half his size, but the stranger said he could have never got him in the car without me. He was lying, of course, but I'll always remember how good that made me feel.

The old car jumped and spun here and there, but it pulled those hills eventually and dad was in the hospital about two hours after he had fallen. He had broken ribs and cuts and bruises, but the doctor said he would be just fine in a few weeks.

The local newspaper carried a front page story of the incident, and the title read, "Larry to The Rescue". I knew it gave me a little too much credit, but it felt good to read that someone thought I was an eleven-year-old hero.

I asked dad if he really thought I was a hero and he thought about it awhile. Then he said, no, I wasn't. He said that if I had really been a hero, I would have caught him when he fell. And then he grinned and winced and said it hurt something awful when he laughed. And as thankful as I was that dad was all-right, it hurt me quite a bit too. With him laid up so long, I'd be all of twelve years old before I got to hunt ducks again!

But I took a couple of trips that fall with my grandpa, and the following October, dad decided I was old enough to start hunting with my own gun. For my birthday, I received a single-shot, second-hand Iver-Johnson shotgun, a break-

I pose with my dad and his cousin, Charlie. I was 12, hunting with my old Iver-Johnson. The Big Piney harbored lots of ducks back then, but the ones I killed were all on the water.

open 16-gauge that hadn't been used much. I've owned some fine sporting shotguns since then, but I've never been more proud of any of them than I was of that old 16-gauge. And on my first trip dad paddled me up close to a flock of wood ducks sitting on a log. When he whispered an O.K., I squeezed the trigger. Two beautiful drakes were left on the water, and in that day, you were only allowed one wood-duck. Technically, I was a violator on my first trip. We didn't shoot at any more wood ducks that day, but there were some teal and mallards. That fall, I killed a dozen or so ducks and every one was sitting on the water.

I didn't consider whether or not it was sporting to shoot a sitting duck. I was just a kid, and I wanted to kill something. As the years went on, my dad taught me a reverence for life far and above just defining sportsmanship. But youngsters at that age are not very proficient with a shotgun, and even though I shot at the ducks which jumped up before our john-boat, I never got one. The sitting ones had a fairly good chance of getting away too, but some didn't, and I started learning to shoot that old Iver-Johnson.

Like the river that passed by as the old john-boat covered the miles each fall, so did the years, and by the time I was fiften years old, I started taking my turn at paddling the boat while dad hunted. By then I had a pump gun, a model-twelve Winchester twelve-gauge. And by then, I had

By the age of 14, I was a veteran. With my dad and uncle Bryce, I pose with another limit from the Piney. By then, I shot a Model 12 pump gun and had learned to hit ducks in flight.

10

learned to shoot ducks on the wing. That fall I dropped my first banded wood duck out of a flock we flushed beneath a group of river oaks. I found out that the drake woodie had been banded the year before in Wisconsin. I remember carrying that band with me as if it were gold, and I was fascinated by the fact that those flocks of ducks passing through the Ozarks had come from places like Wisconsin and Minnesota and North Dakota and even Canada. Those seemed to be lands so far away and mysterious, surely wilderness spots like the writers in Outdoor Life so often described. I dreamed of seeing those far-off lands, but it didn't seem likely. I hadn't been out of Missouri yet. But the ducks came to us each fall, and that was good enough. Heaven, I was sure, could be no more beautiful than the Big Piney in November.

Something happened that fall that I will remember forever. We were floating the lower portion of the river as the weather was changing. The cold had moved in and a norther was on its way. There were new mallards in, the northern mallards with bright red legs, and flocks that numbered 20 or 30, instead of the three or four or five you would find earlier in the fall.

We spotted a big flock in the middle of the river, and dad began to paddle up on them, aided by a wind behind us that pushed us along, catching the blind on the front of the boat and making it into a sail. We were no longer just piling boughs on the front of our john-boat. My dad and one of his friends had developed a wire frame which attached to the front of the boat and woven wire within it held the boughs and limbs to create a better blind than grandpa had ever been able to use. It came up to about eye-level and stuck out several feet both ways to hide the boat and the paddles. To waterfowl and other wildlife on the river, it just appeared to be a brush-pile floating downstream. As long as you kept the boat from turning sideways, you were hidden.

That day, we hugged the bank as we floated closer and

closer, and were hidden from above by some overhanging maples. We were only about 50 yards from the flock when we heard ducks high above us, calling to the group on the water. Several old hens answered, and dad backed the boat in against the bank out of the wind so that we could watch. There were two or three flocks in the air, and they were circling and losing altitude to join the mallards on the water. I watched another flock sweep in over the top of the high bluff just down river, and bank and spiral down. The flocks passing over us made chuckling sounds I had never heard before, and the wind from their wings seemed to roar as they swept above. And then I watched them fall into the eddy before us like snowflakes out of a winter storm, the cupped wings, the extended bright legs, green heads glistening in the sunlight. They side-slipped and funneled from above, dropping in until it seemed the river was covered with mallards, quacking and splashing and calling to the last of the incoming flocks still above us.

I had never seen anything so beautiful, so hypnotic and spectacular. Nothing I had witnessed on the river had ever rendered me so spellbound, so filled with amazement. Dad and I took several drakes from the last flock to descend before us, and as our shotguns roared, a hundred mallards or more took to flight. For the first time, I had witnessed the sight of ducks over decoys, even though the decoys were live. I didn't know how often I would see that sight in years to come, because I had no idea that I would ever hunt ducks over decoys. But that day, at the age of fifteen, I was hooked. Duck hunting was in my blood, and would always be. Sometime soon, I would see the rest of it... the calling, the placing decoys, the training of a good Labrador. But all my life I would see those first flocks sweeping out of the graying skies over that bluff towering above the Piney, and hear the sound of their wings cutting the air above us as they came down. That day, my obsession with duck-hunting became stronger than ever.

Upper left: Dad and a college friend drop wood ducks from behind our floating blind in 1968. Above: Dad stands beside our wooden john boat with the frame of the blind attached. Left: A better look at the blind, with boughs attached.

Old Rambunctious when he was young.

Chapter 3

The Best There Ever Was

There are many things about the fall of 1992 that I am not likely to forget. For one thing, it became apparent that old Rambunctious could not hunt much longer. My old Labrador was almost ten years old, and what hurt the most was, he still wanted to get out there and get 'em as much as ever. But he had been to Canada with us in early October, and it was plain to see that he couldn't do what he wanted to do. The arthritis was setting in, and his health was failing with age.

In western Missouri, the fall of '92 marked the beginning of the big floods which continued until late summer of '93, and in November of that year, Truman reservoir was about as high as it could get. Water backed way up into crop fields that couldn't be harvested, and into the timbered creeks where the acorn crop had been tremendous. There were thousands and thousands of acres of milo, wheat, popcorn and sunflower standing in water, and by mid-November it looked as if every duck in the Midwest had found the sprawling reservoir.

Truman Lake attracts numbers of duck-hunters who aren't ready to hunt that type of water. It always has, and when the water is low, the duck hunting may not be very good. Sometimes you'll see hunters arrive from out-of-state who heard how good it was a year or two before, and they find the lake at normal stage with just a normal amount of waterfowl. When it's ten or fifteen feet above normal, it can be a duck hunters paradise. In the fall of '92 it was 20 some feet above normal, and paradise wasn't quite sufficient language to describe it.

15

Hunters were thick as flies, but most of them congregated in the same areas they always hunted, not far from the nearest boat landing. Over the years I've noticed that most of those hunters who come regularly have blinds built on their boats which keep them from traveling very far, and make them stick out like a sea-gull on a sand bar. Some use plywood, and some use wire, and they cover that with weeds, or cedar boughs or burlap and go to the same place year after year. Several years back, such a boat blind got too far out in the open water and a winter squall caught them and swamped the top-heavy boat. Three men died.

My boat is made to cover big water, and the blind isn't put in place until I get where I want to hunt. I sometimes take it into areas where no one else can go, and that's what we were doing in the fall of '92. We found ducks way up a small creek about six or eight miles from everyone else, where flooded timber next to a milo field gave ducks a great place to loaf and feed. We found it one Monday afternoon when the weather was calm and cool and the skies clear. With two dozen decoys on the water, we had a limit of nine ducks in about 20 minutes, and took movies the rest of the afternoon.

We planned to return the next morning and hunt another pocket a short distance away... an opening in flooded timber, where it was easy to hide the boat, and the sun would be right for good photos.

There were three of us. Mike Dodson, who I had hunted with for fifteen years or so, is a fire-fighter from Harrison, Arkansas who would rather hunt ducks than eat... and he loves to eat, ducks in particular. Rich Abdoler is a Corps of Engineers Ranger on Truman Lake, who risks his marriage every year to take his vacation during the duck season. As a result, the three of us hunt waterfowl from Canada to Arkansas most years, from late September to mid-January on occasion, and we have become very close friends because of it. There isn't a one of us who wouldn't help the other one kill his limit if the law would allow it. And that became the topic of a rather heated debate that Monday afternoon in November as we gathered to clean ducks and plan for the following morn. It seemed to Rich and me that Mike, who is something of a game hog due to his Arkansas nature, was not nearly as selective as he should have been in his shooting. To be specific, he had touched off a round after, by our figuring, his limit was on the water. Mike denied it, saying that if he had erred at all, it was in

Mike Dodson, above, and Rich Abdoler, calling.

helping to bring down a mallard drake which Rich had merely crippled. That didn't set well with Rich, who is sensitive about the fact that he is not nearly as good a wing shot as Mike and I, though he has never formally conceded the fact. Actually he denies it completely!

For awhile, it appeared that if we hunted the next day at all, it would be in three different areas. Finally I said that

I intended to take photo's while the two of them limited out, and I would load my gun only after Mike had his limit in hand and his gun in his case. And furthermore, should he drop one more duck than the law allowed I would turn him in to the nearest conservation agent. Mike took offense, and replied that he would take only three shells with him the following day, at which Rich and I scoffed heartily. And that's when the whole idea of the Greater Truman Duck Hunting Championship originated.

Finally we would answer the questions each of us had secretly asked for such a long time...was Mike indeed a throbbing gizzard of a game hog? Could Rich actually kill a duck without shooting it in the decoys? Would either of the two hunt with me if I didn't own the boat?

We were there at dawn the next morning, the three of us and old Ram the Labrador. Several thousand ducks left as we arrived, and finally, as shooting hours approached, we had 30 decoys on the water, and layers of ducks above us funneling down into the opening in the timber.

We flipped coins, and Mike won, so he got the first chance. The first flock was his, and he would be allowed only one shot. Rich would be next, and I would shoot last, each of us allowed only one shot per flock. When a limit for each hunter was reached, the champion would be the one who shot the fewest number of shells. The winner would be the undisputed 'best there ever was'. Killing a hen of any species would count as an extra shot, as would any shells used to dispatch cripples. Despite the fact that Mike is a game hog, and Rich has been known to shoot ducks only an inch or so above the water, none of us tolerate the killing of hens. It's a matter of pride. It will happen on occasion, but it's a rare occasion, and never is a hen mallard killed intentionally.

Mike had an easy task. With mallards practically in his lap, he fired once and a greenhead lay belly-up in the blocks not 25 yards away. Rich had only a few minutes to wait, before another flock zeroed in on us and circled the treetops. Half of them settled outside the decoys, but one drake and a pair of hens drifted in on cupped wings near Rich's end of the boat, and the greenhead was a dead duck... literally.

Ram was beside himself, restrained on a leash to keep him in the boat, and I couldn't stand to see him so tempted without letting him retrieve a duck. We let him go, and the old dog gave it his all, returning with Mike's mallard. We helped him in the boat, and he stood there too tired to shake off the water which poured from his coat, trembling from fatigue. I wouldn't let him go after the other one. Maybe later we could arrange a shallow water retrieve.

My two hunting partners sympathized with the old dog, but wasted no such compassion for me. They took a great deal of satisfaction in the fact that I was under some degree of pressure shooting last. I worked the biggest flock of all, and as I sighted down my gun barrel, there were a half dozen drake mallards hovering over our set. But there were some widgeons in that funneling flock, and I picked out a drake baldpate that was beautifully colored and within range above the mallards. I knew before I pulled the trigger that the shot would be good, and the widgeon tumbled from the skies as the rest of the flock fought for altitude. I had the edge now, with the third duck of my limit, since only two of the three could be mallards back then.

In the next thirty minutes, Mike picked up his "extra" duck by dropping an immature pintail drake that came in with fifteen or twenty mallards. Rich followed with his second drake mallard and when it was my turn, I swung on two drake mallards which swept wide and sailed into range just taking a look at the decoys. I shouldn't have risked it, but I did, and the lead greenhead folded neatly at the gun blast. So far, we had dropped six ducks with six shots. And now, something that had started out as half-hearted competition for the fun of it, was turning into a serious shooting match.

Mike had the upper hand, needing a drake mallard to

finish out, and no time to think about missing. With six or seven ducks over the decoys, he carefully chose his last shot, and with a final drake plunging stone dead into the floodwaters before us, he unloaded his gun with a smug look of defiance.

Rich could take no more mallards, and he had to pass up two or three flocks before he had a chance at his third duck. It wasn't an easy shot, but he made it, picking off a drake widgeon as it flared above the decoys behind sever-

With his limit, Mike and Ram watch asRich goes for his final duck.

al mallards which had hit the water briefly and sprang back into flight. Now we had eight ducks with eight shots, and it was my turn. Despite the cool morning, there were beads of sweat on my forehead. I scarcely heard my comrades calling pleadingly to a new flock, scarcely noticed my trembling Labrador looking anxiously to the skies where red-legged mallards were descending like leaves from a summer whirlwind. It had come down to this, a final shot to determine if I would be able to show my face at Peggy's Restaurant that afternoon, where my hunting partners would be quick to point out that I had ruined a perfect morning on the marsh. If it came to that, I could sit in the pick-up and go without coffee! There was a rush of wings, and mallards all around us. I could hear Mike whispering to Rich, "What's he waiting for?" It was now or never!

I snapped the stock to my shoulder, picked a green head from the descending flock and squeezed the trigger as my barrel crossed his path. In only seconds it seemed, they were gone, dozens of mallards that had been intent on loafing there in the acorn-filled backwaters of the Truman Lake tributary, now hastily retreating from sight toward the distant horizon, scarcely visible through the maze of branches. All of them but one! I have never breathed a bigger sigh of relief... my mallard floated stone dead among the decoys.

We sat there for a moment, savoring the moment, the best of friends once again, having figured out a way to keep Mike honest, with all of us surprised that any of us could have killed three ducks with three shots.

But it was a bittersweet triumph, because we all knew without saying it that it was my old Labradors last trip. Since retrieving that first duck, he had sat beside me straining at a leash which kept him in the boat while he watched ducks splashing into the decoys less than 30 yards away. For so many years there had been the four of us. You just had to count old Ram. On long trips he had stretched out in the back seat of my extended cab pick-up, knowing that he would be called upon to find the cripples and make the longest of retrieves. All the way to Canada or Nebraska or Iowa, you never knew he was there.

The old chocolate Lab had never been a perfect dog... I don't suppose he would have won any ribbons, and I didn't care. Despite the fact that he couldn't stay put until I sent him, Ram was my dog, and I loved him, and I think Rich and Mike did too. There were many ducks over the years which he retrieved that we would not have found. There were memories of great hunts, times when he found cripples underwater, the day he broke through ice to disappear beneath an undercut bank in pursuit of a crippled mallard. I thought he was a goner that day, but after a full 30 seconds he came back out with the mallard in his mouth.

Ram sat beside my desk when I worked, and from the front porch he watched over my daughters at play when they were young. During the fall he hunted pheasants and ruffed grouse and prairie grouse, ducks and geese. There were so many memories, and now I knew we were down to the very last one.

And so I let him go once more, for one last retrieve, one last duck. He had several on the water to choose from, and he got the easiest one, a drake mallard that had floated out away from the blocks. When he got it, he didn't come right back, he waded out to a little mud flat and just stood there for a moment, catching his wind. Mike and Rich said we ought to go get him, but I stopped them. Ram was enjoying it. He stayed there for awhile, with ducks in the air above him and decoys bobbing ever so slightly in the sun. And he savored the moment, as I was doing, remembering.

We helped him back in the boat, and I guess I never praised him more for so little. It was a great day, a great hunt.... the way it should be for a great dogs last retrieve.

There never was a declared winner in the Greater

Ozarks Duck Shooting Championship, by the way. We intended to continue it the next morning, but we hunted a different spot that day, and before we agreed on the shooting order, a flock of ringnecks came whistling in over our blocks and caught us by surprise. As those bluebills often do, they swung out over the lake and circled back for a second look, and three shotguns roared in unison as they returned. Six or seven shotshell hulls hit the floor of the boat, and when the action was over, one ringneck lay on his back, kicking feebly at the sky. Whoever dropped that one blackjack out of that squadron of jets is unarguably the champion duck hunter... .but we have no idea which one of us it was!

I hope that once again this fall we will be trying to determine just which of the three of us is the best there ever was, somewhere where there are backwaters teeming with ducks. I have a great Labrador to hunt with, a grandson of Rambunctious, and the spitting image of the old dog, with lot's of spirit, and lots of ability. His grandpa is gone now, he died peacefully one morning in the summer of 1993, and he rests now beneath the oaks and hickories beside the kennel where younger dogs carry on his lineage. With him is the English Setter, Freckles, who was his best friend and pheasant hunting partner, and who died a few months before he did. In his last days, he doddered around my house on arthritic legs and hunted field mice, and I believe he was a happy old dog 'til the very end.

It hurt a great deal to see him go, but I feel lucky to have owned such a companion and to have been rewarded with all those hunts which some hunters only dream of. And every time a flock of ducks circles high above my decoys, I feel like he's there in spirit, watching it all, still trembling with excitement and anticipation.

Indeed, Ram will live on as long as Mike and Rich and I hunt ducks, and as long as he has grandsons and great grandsons to continue the tradition. And it is fitting that his last trip and his last retrieve took place on that glorious day in the fall of '92, when the hunting was as good as it can get.. .maybe the best there ever was for us. The old dog deserved that kind of a finish, because as far as I'm concerned he really is "the best there ever was."

Chapter 4

A Good Spread of Decoys

I was just out of college, and working with a pair of young wildlife management students who were whiz-bang duck-callers.. .about the best I've ever hunted with. They took me duck hunting in one of their best places, up Point Remove Creek just off the Arkansas River to flooded crop fields known as the Blackwell Bottoms.

The limit was four mallard drakes per day, under the point system drakes were 25 points, and hens 70. We'd hunt an entire season and never kill a hen. On my first trip with them, a lone drake came in just after shooting hours and circled to look over our decoys. When he passed over the second time he was about 40 yards high and I dropped him. My partners congratulated me on a good shot, then explained that duck hunting their way was something different than the pass shooting I had gotten use to at Missouri's public areas while in college. You waited until ducks decoyed....when they had wings cupped and legs out, settling into the blocks at 30 yards, completely fooled. And shortly afterward, I saw what they meant, after they had called and pleaded with a flock of ten or twelve wary mallards which had already seen their share of hunting pressure in states to the north. It must have taken ten minutes and a dozen passes as those ducks worked the decoys, and my partners pulled them back and in finally with duck-calling artistry. I've hunted with a few hunters since then who never learned what I did that first day in Arkansas. Waterfowl hunting, whether ducks or geese, is not pass shooting, it is decoying.... taking the shots when, and only when, the ducks are fooled and committed to the decoys.

Enjoying that type of hunting is the product of several factors, one of them being the placement and use of decoys. How many you need to use depends on the time of the season, the water you are hunting and the competition or hunting pressure. It's almost never the same from one day to another, or from one place to another, and it isn't something you can learn by reading about it.

No matter how much you hear or you read, you have to hunt ducks and experience the successes and failures to get a feel for using decoys properly. And that's what it is, not a knowledge or set of rules, but a feel.. an understanding of what ducks are and what they do. I won't try at all to tell anyone how to use a duck call in this book because it is next to impossible to do that with written words. Good callers learn about that feel...as much when to call and how to call by watching the response of the flocks. You can make the most perfect call there is and flare ducks by not knowing when to use it. You get a feel for that as you become an experienced hunter, and only experience can make an effective duck-caller. The best callers never go to the calling contests and championships. They are men who hunt, and you don't call when hunting like the people do in those contests. Calling is dependent on conditions and situations. I don't call ducks in flooded timber on Truman Lake like I do on Netley Marsh or the grain field potholes of Manitoba. And how I call, depends on what the ducks are doing. Approaching, swinging, passing directly above, heading away.....all those elicit a different response with a duck call. And sometimes, it's wisest to call very, very little. If you want to learn to call ducks, find an experienced hunter and listen to him call. Hunt with duck-callers who have lots of years behind them. And of course, that's the best way to learn to use decoys too!

Believe it or not, duck decoys were used in north America long before there were any firearms. Early explorers wrote about how certain North American Indians lured waterfowl into nets and traps with decoys made from reeds and clay. And on occasions, archaeologists have unearthed just such decoys in excavations.

Sometime in the early 1800's hunters along the New England coast began using decoys carved from blocks of white pine. Even in the heyday of the market hunter, when live wing-clipped ducks were used, wooden decoys were added to create the attraction of greater numbers. Companies began to mass produce wooden decoys in the 1870's and for about 50 years, millions were produced for about two dollars per dozen. If you have some of those decoys, especially the ones with brand names and dates imprinted or etched on the bottom, you have a real collectors item, possibly worth a good deal of money.

Live decoys were outlawed in the 1930's, and hard plastic, cork and paper-mache' decoys became popular about then. Next came inflatable rubber decoys and eventually the flexible hard plastic blocks we have today. Frankly, I can't see how decoys can get much better than they are now.

Of course they still make cork decoys, and it is said they are the best ever used.. .but they are very expensive. One thing for sure, having the best decoys won't do you much good if you don't use them properly.

Some duck hunters can't get enough decoys when hunting on open water, especially when there's a lot of competition. As much as hunters love to brag on their calling, most know that very often a good set of decoys in the right place will draw more ducks than the world's greatest caller in the wrong spot with a smaller set, unless of course we are talking about hunting timber, where just the opposite is true.

Competition that requires you to use a large number of decoys doesn't always come from other hunters. There have been times when rafts of ducks in open water made unattractive the six or seven dozen decoys set close to a hunter's blind. When you get a situation where large groups of live ducks are sitting down in open water, you are going to have a tough time competing with them, and you'd better have some numbers and the right wind directions.

In most situations however, two or three dozen decoys will do the job and sometimes great pothole hunting can be enjoyed with only eight or ten decoys. Hunting in flooded timber usually doesn't require many decoys at all, because you are bringing ducks in with a call. They don't see your

blocks at a distance, they sight a small group of decoys as they pass over, and a dozen is adequate to bring them down if your calling is good. In the tall flooded timber, you'd better know what duck calling is about..

When you find the right place and there are no other hunters, a few decoys can draw great flocks of course. But then again, there are times on open marshes when five or six dozen decoys are necessary. When you are hunting big waters with wide open spaces around you, and perhaps other hunters not all that far away, a big spread is important. On public hunting areas like those operated by the Missouri Department of Conservation, where blinds are placed strategically throughout a marsh, I don't even consider less than five or six dozen decoys. In a small lake in the sandhills of Nebraska, or in a Manitoba grain field pothole I'll use less than two dozen. In a small slough off an Ozarks river, six or eight decoys will be plenty. It's true that at times, inexperienced waterfowlers will scatter so many decoys they hurt their chances. When flocks land at the edge of a set, and those decoys are at the outer edge of shotgun range, the hunter is in trouble. Widely scattered decoys won't concentrate the incoming ducks where you want them for effective shooting.

Of course there are no rules that are carved in granite when it comes to duck hunting. I remember hunting in a small shallow pothole in a grain field years ago when we filled it so full of decoys you couldn't throw a rock without hitting one and the incoming mallards still hovered over them, trying to find a place to sit.

Remember that as a rule, it is best not to place your decoys in a tight bunch. A tightly-grouped wad of ducks usually is alarmed and preparing for flight. Loafing feeding ducks are usually scattered helter-skelter and facing all directions. Ducks with heads up, all facing the same direction, are usually alarmed or nervous about something.

What's most important is remembering to leave pockets or holes in your pattern which bring the ducks to the exact spot you want them.. Decoy patterns, in which your blocks are used to form a hook or a "J" or a "V" are effective in channeling ducks to an open area which is the perfect range for waiting shotguns.

When you've finished placing decoys, try to separate any which are clicking together in the wind, or several decoys clumped together. Remove any decoys which are leaking and listing to the side or sinking.

Old timers will tell you that an early season spread of decoys should have 70 or 80 percent hens while late season spreads should have 50 or 60 percent drakes. This is because early season flocks usually have fewer brightly colored drakes and flocks in December or January have so many more. That's true in the northern half of the country, but not in the south. When the season opens in Canada, young drakes are just beginning to look like drakes, and older drakes are certainly not yet brightly colored. With some of those flocks, green heads and white rings just aren't discernible. But ducks arriving in Arkansas at the beginning of the season are in bright plumage.

So those rules the old duck hunters went by... would a flock of mallards actually be drawn to or repelled by a set of decoys with too many or too few drakes? I'm doubtful, but most of those old veteran hunters killed a lot more ducks in their day than I have in mine.

I remember, in my early days as an outdoor writer, doing articles for magazines about decoy sets, and I would, as they asked me to do, write about all the patterns used to fool ducks. The old sporting magazines when I was a youngster and well before, did lots of those features, and they sure looked good. Then we'd be out there hunting and it would be cold and windy and the boat would be blowing around or the mud would be pulling your waders off your feet and no one would give a second thought to patterns. Shooting hours would be ten minutes away and we'd be trying to get the decoys in the water.. .to heck with patterns.

But no matter what, we learned to pay attention to the

outer edge of our blocks, and to leave those landing areas, or openings, for ducks to alight in. And we learned to consider the placement of those decoys according to where we would be shooting from, and the wind which would determine approach. If you get a handle on those factors, you've got it figured out. Few hunters will form perfect patterns when shooting hours are near and there's wind and

cold and mud to contend with. In such situations, think of that landing space, or hole, and don't let the edge of your decoy set drift too far from your gun, or you'll have ducks alighting just out of range. Wary ducks late in the season often light out into the lake and join rafts of live waterfowl by swimming in to join them. They have a tendency to do that with your decoys if you let the outer edge of your blocks get too far out, and too loosely set.

Setting proper decoy spreads is not all you need to be aware of. Because ducks land into the wind, you don't want the wind in your face. If you are looking over open water, you'd like to have the wind at your back. This causes incoming ducks to approach straight at you, so you have to be well hidden. Don't let the placement of your decoys call attention to your blind. Ducks coming straight into your blind will often see you, especially if there's any sunlight hitting you. I know that ducks eyes are set on the side of the head, but if they are coming directly at you, they have more time to be looking and they are looking at you for too long.

Actually, many duck hunters prefer a wind from the right because it brings ducks in from the left. And in looking at the spread, they are not looking past it toward you. You are at the side, away from the spread which is the center of their attention. Ducks approaching from the left is a perfect situation if you are a right-handed shotgunner, and it keeps the ducks from seeing you as easily at a distance. But you can't always set up as you would prefer.. you are at the mercy of the wind, and the wind dictates your decoy spread.

If a wind change causes your decoys to be in the wrong place for approaching ducks, you'll be ahead to move everything. It really irks me to have a wind change just after dawn and have to get out in the decoys and start rearranging everything while ducks are flying, but there's little use in fighting the wind. If a wind change affects my hunting adversely, I change everything, even to a point of picking up and moving to another area. I do that because of those days from long ago when I said to heck with it, I'm not moving... and then went home with no ducks.

Remember that ducks hesitate to approach over a fringe of trees, or high cover of any kind, especially after they've been hunted awhile. That's why a wind change can ruin you... it causes ducks to change the approach to your decoys. I have had times when everything was perfect except the ducks continually shied away because they didn't want to come in over a fringe of ten-foot bushes. They like to circle over an open body of water or a low grassy marsh when they can. They may ignore those willows or low trees early in the season if you are hunting up north, but as the season progresses, they begin to become much warier, and they don't like to pass over places where a hunter could be hiding.

And then there are those days when you can throw the rules out the window; days when a blizzard is bearing down from the north and tired, incoming flights drop into the decoys from high altitudes despite surrounding vegetation or wind direction. Sure, I've seen the times when you could throw away the rule book, even times when ducks dropped into decoys with a wind rather than against it. But usually, that isn't the way it happens.

Usually, how you set decoys in regard to your surroundings will dictate the success of your hunt. Old, weathered, beat-up decoys should be culled or repainted. I've seen ducks flare from decoys quite often, and that should never happen. If a decoy doesn't look like a duck, get rid of it. And remember that those days when it's so still that a dead gnat causes a ripple will make poor-looking decoys look like a warning sign.

In fact, nothing hurts duck hunting like a still day. That's why some hunters use underwater stakes with hooks in the top to pass a line from decoys to their blind. If you can keep a couple of decoys bobbing a little, you can make a spread look a little better. Other hunters use battery operated propellor-driven swimming decoys to give life to a stone-still spread. I don't use either. I did a little of that when I was younger, but it's too much effort for the results I have seen. Other hunters would argue that. When I'm hunting from chest waders on still days, standing up against a tree, I keep kicking the water to create a disturbance approaching ducks can see. But you don't do that when ducks are working your decoys unless you are very well hidden.

Inspect your anchors and anchor lines on decoys periodically. Check the knots and be sure there are no worn places in the line. If you have bell type anchors, you can keep anchor lines from unwinding and becoming entangled by attaching 1-inch cross-sections of old bicycle inner tubes to the line beside the anchors, to be pulled over the heads like large rubber bands. Of course, there are those wrappable lead weights which can be wrapped around the neck of the decoy, and if you can afford a few dozen of those, you need nothing else.

Because of the variety of waters I might hunt in a season, I have fought with decoy strings all my years as a duck hunter. I usually hunt water where a five-foot decoy string is adequate, but then there will be times when I need fifteen feet of line. You can conquer this problem by attaching twelve or fifteen feet of anchor line, and attaching a trotline clip at the back of the keel. Use that clip to shorten the line to the depth you want to hunt the next day. There's no use playing out fifteen feet of line if you are hunting in a marsh with water only fifteen inches deep. Many hunters may never need fifteen feet of line, but the way I hunt, I sometimes do.

And use a dark brown anchor line if you can. Never use white nylon or bright green or black if you are hunting occasionally in very clear water, as I often do. Of course if you are hunting muddy or colored water, the lines won't show and it won't make much difference.

It's smart to put your name on the bottom of your

decoys with marker, and maybe a phone number. If another duck hunter finds a couple of your decoys, he might just return them if he has a number to call. But usually it is done to keep good friends from becoming enemies when one winds up with more decoys than he ever had and the other has less.

My two good friends, Mike Dodson and Rich Abdoler would often set out decoys together when we hunted ducks, and each had their name on the bottom of each decoy they owned. Maybe the best joke I ever pulled on them was the day I took a black marker out in the marsh, and every time I got a chance, I would cross out one name and write in the other. By the end of the day, I had blacked out and replaced names on a dozen decoys or better. When the two of them started sorting decoys that night, each thought the other one was trying to get his decoys. Eventually they blamed me, as they always did when anything went wrong.

In closing, remember that the best place to learn to hunt ducks is out there in the cold and the wet and the mud. That's where you'll eventually learn to use decoys, and learn to call, and learn to shoot.. and learn who your real friends are.

Chapter 5

Aladdin's Story

We were at the edge of a harvested corn field... no decoys, no blind, no waders. Hundreds of mallards were coming into the field before the snow fell. I stood beneath a huge old hedge tree and called flocks of 30 or 40 ducks over me, picking out the biggest, prettiest drakes of the bunch as they swung around the field borders. I don't know if there is a sight in nature that is equal to that of a flock of mallards descending from the heights on cupped wings, sideslipping to lose altitude, and sweeping overhead with a rush of wind over wings only 30 yards above the ground.

It was the last day of the season, and I lead one last mallard drake just right, squeezing off a final salute to a great year. The drake never knew what hit him, and he folded neatly, plummeting to the earth only a short distance away, filling my limit. Lad sat beside me trembling with aniticipation, and I let him make his last retrieve of his first season.

Lad, short for Aladdin, (never let your daughter name your dog) was a year old in the fall of '94. I remember well his first hunt. It took place in September of that year. The rain had finally come to our part of the Ozarks, and the weekend was to be much cooler. I got a call from Corps of Engineers Ranger, Rich Abdoler, who said he had seen hundreds of teal on Truman Lake, and wanted to go out at dawn to hunt. I talked him into an evening hunt instead, and late Sunday afternoon we were setting out a dozen decoys without a teal in sight. It was the last day, though, and we needed to be there.

Actually in September of '94 Lad was only eight months old. He looked older, but there was a lot of puppy left in that

39

big brown body. In the lawn, he was doing great, going after singles or doubles and acting as if he would be the spitting image of old Rambunctious. Rambunctious, was the best Labrador I've owned. In fact, in his prime, Ol' Ram was the third or fourth greatest Labrador in the world. I learned years ago to never say my dog was the best dog in the world, because it always starts an argument. Every other Labrador owner and duck hunter thinks his dog is the best in the whole world, too. But no one argues that his dog is the third or fourth best dog in the world, so I can claim mine is and no one says a thing. And if you think about it, being third or fourth in the whole world isn't bad. I wouldn't mind being the third or fourth best looking man in the world, or the third or fourth best athlete or even the third or fourth richest man in the world. Would you? Now you are beginning to see what I mean.

That September, Ram was thirteen years old and having trouble getting around. He didn't much care for the young dog, and he let him know it. Lad was lucky to have both ears by the time he was a year old.

But anyway, back to the first hunt, there on that September afternoon on that shallow Truman Lake marsh. Rich thought we were wasting our time. It had warmed up again, and the only thing flying was cormorants and mosquitoes. But the water was up just a bit, and wild millet, nutsedge and smartweed was plentiful, providing excellent food for wild ducks. We pulled the 19-foot square-stern canoe into the vegetation, which stuck up about two feet, and provided a suitable hiding place, since teal are not as wary as other species.

Rich and I were talking about hunting experiences from years past, and speculating on how good the duck-hunting might be if we could get a two or three-foot rise on Truman that fall, with such an abundance of vegetation growing to the waters edge. About that time, I caught a glimpse of a low-flying flock of ducks wheeling around from behind us, blue wing panels flashing in the sunlight. They quickly set their wings, approaching into the wind over open water. There were about 20 in all, and I dumped my first teal in the decoys before Rich opened up. I missed the second shot, but swung on a pair of birds retreating to my left and dropped both with one shot. Rich had two down, and it was a great opportunity for Lad's first lesson. Beside himself with excitement, he brought back a decoy!

I waded out with him to the last two birds I had dropped, and he gingerly picked one up... then dropped it. So I tossed one out aways for him, and he got the idea, eagerly retrieving it. Then Rich called him to get his teal, and the pup charged them like a veteran, while I proudly took photo's. With the duck in his mouth however, Lad decided to make the most of it, and he passed Rich, heading ashore to toss the duck in the air and chase it. I'm glad old Ram wasn't there to see it!

Within fifteen minutes, we called to a new flock out over the lake, and they came rocketing over the decoys in only a matter of seconds. The young dog saw the ducks coming this time, and got a good look at a teal which folded over the decoys, splashing down only 30 yards away, stone dead. This time, he didn't hesitate! He charged out in a spray of water, picked up the teal and had to be chased around the boat before he'd give it up.

We paddled back into a golden sunset, confident that there would be good waterfowling when the regular season opened, but not so confident we'd have a hunting dog to retrieve 'em. Just before the new season began, a dog trainer visited my home. He said he had heard that I raised good Labradors, and he was looking for a young Lab to develop as a drug dog. Lad was the one he was really interested in, and he offered me nearly $800. for the nine-month old pup. I had other young Labs I could work with, and I kept remembering that September teal hunt. I knew that as a drug dog, Aladdin would live in style, and become a valuable dog. But still, it really hurt to see him go. My wife and daughter were against it, and there were some tears shed

41

that evening. But they understood it was a decision which would be best for us, and for Lad. He would have a great life.

I heard, during the duck season of 1995, that Lad was doing well and had been promoted to working in schools, giving demonstrations to students concerning the use of dogs in drug detection. He was being given lots of attention, and sleeping beside the bed every night, going everywhere his trainer went. But darn I missed him. I still felt like he was my pup and I wished I hadn't sold him but it was too late to think that way. So I worked with other young dogs, and kept hearing myself say, "I wish he was more like Lad."

In the summer of '96 that trainer who bought him called to tell me he was getting married and leaving his profession for something else. He and his new wife would be moving to the west coast, and she had a small child. She didn't want a Labrador in the house. He wondered if I wanted Aladdin back, at no cost. He said he could sell the big chocolate Lab for some good money, but he wanted to be sure his work partner continued to sleep by the bed, go everywhere I went, and get to hunt ducks until he was old and fat. I was on my way before the phone hit the hook!

I like to believe the young Lab remembered me. He rode back home lying in the front seat of my pick-up with his head beside my leg, then sat up to watch the countryside near home as if he knew where we were going. He had grown to about 90 pounds and the puppy was gone. In its place was a well-tempered, well-trained and intelligent Labrador. I know old Rambunctious would have been proud of him.

In his thirteen years, Ram had sired about 350 puppies for me and other Lab owners. His descendants were exceptional dogs, and I shouldn't have been surprised that Lad was so much like him. But the last time I had taken this youngster on a duck hunt in1994 he had romped all over the marsh with a blue-winged teal in his mouth while flocks flared above our decoys and I yelled threats which would have caused the humane society to wince. I figured we had a lot of hunting to do before Aladdin deserved to be called a hunting dog. And to tell the truth, as glad as I was to have him back, I didn't know what to expect out there in the marsh.

Rich Abdoler and Ram, the grandfather of Aladdin.

So he went with Rich and I to Canada to hunt geese in October, and we found ducks to be swarming those grain fields in numbers like I have never seen. The first mallard of the season went down in a small pothole, and Lad charged out to get it as if he remembered all about this duck-hunting stuff. Except this time he didn't do any victory laps, he just came back and left it at my feet. Moments later he dug a crippled mallard out of a grain swathe which I would have never found.

My partner and I bagged 36 ducks in Manitoba that week and Lad watched most of them fall. When we packed up and headed for the Ozarks, I knew Lad's career as a drug dog was over...his new job was finding ducks and grouse and pheasants, and he liked it.

On Truman Lake, the duck hunting started out fairly good and got better. Aladdin would leave the boat to stand beside me when I hunted in waders, braving the cold water just so he could watch those ducks. He wasn't great on experience, but you couldn't fault his eagerness. As he returned with duck after duck, you could see he finally had it all figured out.

The best day of the year came just before Thanksgiving when we found a milo field on a small lake tributary where there was plenty of grain on the ground. Ducks were alighting on the small creek and walking up into the grain to feed. I spread a dozen decoys on the water, and then built a blind in the milo. Lad sat beside me, comically peering out from beneath the camouflage as flock after flock bore in from over the lake, and responded to the call. I picked out one drake at a time, and each fell in the milo around us. The Lab used his nose to find four mallard drakes and a gadwall that would have been a real problem for me to find in the weeds and standing crops.

So Lad is a veteran now, as he lies here beside the fireplace perhaps dreaming about circling flocks of mallards. He's not old Rambunctious, but he doesn't have to be. He's just as good in most ways, and better in some... the second or third best Labrador in the whole world, I figure.

I guess, come to think of it, I had forgotten the first hunts Ram made, way back there when I was young too. Maybe I had more patience then. Anyway, I'll never give up on another young retriever just because he wants to play with his very first duck.

A Few Words on Selecting and Training a Labrador

I'll be the first to concede that I'm no expert on retrievers, and I'm not a very good dog trainer either. But I've raised a number of Labrador puppies over the past twenty years and I've learned a few things here and there which might be of help to you if you aren't yet an expert either. First of all, Labradors were developed a long time ago primarily to swim out into the cold water off the east coast of Canada to retrieve the tow ropes of ships coming into a harbor. They were developed as heavy-bodied animals with stamina and strength... the body mass to help them take the cold water temperatures. Therefore, they originated as a highly intelligent, heavy dogs in the 80 to 100 pound range, and they were retrievers. I'm sure it didn't take much to get them to retrieve ducks instead of tow ropes.

They were recognized as a distinct breed only about 1904, which is probably about the time they came into their own as duck dogs for market hunters. But Labs weren't the first choice of those commercial hunters who made their living selling ducks. They preferred the Chesapeake Bay Retriever, and with good reason. The Chessie was a very agressive and protective dog, built like a Lab with a longer and wavier coat, and a real attitude. They would sit in the back of a pick-up and guard the whole truck with their lives. If you walked by and looked inside at the contents, you'd best keep your distance. Pick up one of those ducks or decoys and you might lose an arm.

Chessies are a little more powerful than Labs, with somewhat greater stamina...prone to be a one man dog, and darned independent. I remember trying to photograph a Chesapeake Bay Retriever once holding a blue-winged teal.

He'd hold it awhile, and then put it down. His owner kept putting it back in his mouth so I could get more pictures. After three or four times, the dog got tired of it, and he growled menacingly at his owner. The guy patted him on the head and responded, "whatever you say". That's the way it is with Chessies. Individuals I have seen have been friendly and outgoing, but the breed as a whole is made of hardworking, tough, no-nonsense dogs.

The Labrador's popularity has risen from his entirely different attitude. He likes everybody, and if you'll throw a stick for him, he'll go home with you.

The kids can pull his ears, the baby can crawl all over him, and you can yell at him and he'll lick your hand. And he has the nose to find birds with the best of them. Of course, he loves the cold water, and he loves to retrieve.

And remember something, he is a retriever.....the breed was developed for that purpose. I know about the pointing Labs, and you can have them. Some are the results of distant Labrador and German short-hair crosses.

My pointing dog is an English setter, and I have no reason to try to make him into a stock dog. Why would I want my Lab to point? He could never outpoint that setter. But the setter won't charge out in that cold water and swim down a crippled mallard.

Labradors over the years have been bred to be smaller and faster, for the field trial people, and rangier because of the pointing dog ancestry which no one will own up to. The old-style, heavy, blocky hunting dogs are strong and slower, with big, blocky heads and bodies. And they are low-keyed and intelligent, they sit down in a duck blind or a family room and stay put and behave themselves. You may prefer the field trial Labs and the pointing Labs, but I don't. I want the dogs like the ones you saw in the hunting magazines 40 or 50 years ago. I don't have time for field trials and dog shows, my Labs and I spend our time hunting. I don't want any ribbons or trophies, I want days afield and priceless memories.

On those occasions when I use a Lab for pheasant or grouse, I want him to hunt close, flush tight-sitting birds within range, and allow no cripple to escape. A Labrador that points is as unnatural as a coonhound that chases rabbits, and a fast Labrador is about as useful as a fast bassett hound.

I like all three colors of the breed, black, chocolate or

Good Labs come in all colors. This pup will be a real looker.

yellow. You can't know a thing about a Lab's hunting qualities according to his color. In fact, on occasion there will be pups of all three colors from one litter. The chromosome that determines color isn't linked to the ones which determine temperament, nose or the retrieving instinct. You'll be told, by someone who raises yellow Labs, that chocolate dogs have this and that problem, and then perhaps hear, from someone trying to sell you a black puppy, that the yellow dogs are more likely to become blind, or have arthritis or retrieve terrapins instead of ducks, but take all that with a grain of sand or salt or the baloney that it is. I've seen great dogs of all colors and I've seen worthless dogs of all colors. What he will be isn't determined by color. Although I might say that chocolate and yellow labs should not be interbred, because yellow Labs with chocolate parents have a tendency to have the liver pigment in nose and eye-rings. Yellow dogs should retain black noses, so breed yellow to black or black to chocolate if you wish, but don't breed chocolate and yellow.

Don't ever buy a hunter a puppy for a gift unless you know about hunting Labs yourself and what to look for. If distant pedigree means a lot to you, that's fine, but I go by the parents and I couldn't care less how many champions there are in his ancestry. The very best of the Labradors never got into any championships. If the sire and dam are both the kind of Labs I want I'll probably find puppies in their litter I'm really going to like. If a six week old pup carries things around in his mouth, and will chase a rolled up sock a few feet and pick it up, I'm impressed with that kind of puppy. Don't pick a big, fat slow one, and don't pick a runt. Watch for well-built,outgoing, happy, bouncy little pups that run out of the kennel and tug on your shoe-laces. Out of the kennel, he should use his nose as he explores his surroundings, and carry a leaf in his mouth when he comes across it. He should be well-proportioned, with a short, sleek pelt and a blocky, short nose, short ears and otter tail which he holds straight. If you can't see both parents, beware. And if you don't like one of the two, think twice about getting the pup.

Puppies should be wormed at three to four weeks, then again at six weeks. First shots should be given at six to seven weeks, then again at nine weeks and twelve weeks. When he gets his rabies shots at five or six months, he should have a booster to his puppy shots which includes a vaccine against leptosclerosis. And you should get a guarantee against hip displaysia and any other genetic problems. Anyone who sells you a puppy should also give you a thirty day money-back guarantee as long as the puppy is returned healthy. I've always done that, and it gives people who buy a pup from me the assurance that I have confidence in the puppies I raise. And you'll know within thirty days if you've got a puppy you can make into a hunter.

You'll probably have to have a kennel, because you need to keep your dog up when you have to be at work, or can't have him with you. Keep him in it when you have to, but as little as possible. Make the kennel as large and roomy as possible and be sure that at least 60 percent of it is soft ground. Gravel part of it, not all of it. If possible, don't let your Labrador spend one hour of his life on concrete or pavement because those hard surfaces will hurt his joints and muscles. I know it's easier to keep clean, but you spend a day on concrete and you'll understand why I won't have it except for a whelping kennel.

On occasion, a puppy has to be returned. I had one returned when a child was allergic to it, another one was brought back when the new owner found out it wasn't house-broken at seven weeks. She said she didn't know they would pee that often! Both puppies were resold and made fine dogs, although the latter one still has to go every four or five hours.

Pick your puppy and take it home between 45 and 49 days, and immediately begin playing with it if you want a hunting dog. Spend ten minutes each evening rolling an old sock or tennis ball around, and watch how quickly he

49

begins to retrieve. Make him come to you with his prize, don't ever go after him. He'll lose interest quickly when he's young, so don't push it. Quit and try again the next evening. You can take him hunting when he's eight or ten months old and he'll look like a champion on one occasion and a real dud on another. Remember that before he goes out, you have to know that he isn't bothered by a shotgun blast. If he's ready for that, take him.

What makes a good hunting dog of any breed is lots of hunting. A Lab which gets out and watches lots of ducks go down, becomes a good hunting dog if he has anything in him....what you have to teach him to do first is to obey you. Nothing works until that is accomplished. He should come to you on command, sit and stay at least beside you....though young dogs won't stay long when you leave them. Teach him to heel, bring a dummy and drop it at your command. That's all basic stuff that isn't hard to teach him. Teaching him to respond to hand signals and whistles is a great deal more complicated.

I don't think much of sending a good Lab to a trainer, because for every good one there's a half dozen bad ones, and the good ones don't have time for you. The bad ones do! A Lab is so smart, anyone can train a good one. Find some training books and read them thoroughly! I recommend one called TRAINING A RETRIEVER by James Lamb Free, or Richard Wolters' book, WATER DOG. There are others, so read several if you can. Get lots of opinions. I wish I could say more about training a good hunting Labrador, but that's another book, and unfortunately, my Labs become good hunting dogs in spite of me, rather than because of me. But as I said, a dog that gets to go hunting a lot, and sees it all happen, becomes a retriever eventually, if he's got it in him.

I made the mistake of letting old Rambunctious get too old before I started trying to make a new hunting dog to take his place. I did that because Ram didn't like other dogs interfering with his hunting. But when your hunting Labrador reaches eight or nine years old and you begin to see him slow down and age, start a young dog which you can take along. The older dog will help you train him.

Remember, if you can, what I keep forgetting.... It takes awhile to see a young Lab mature and reach his potential. Some of the best take two or three years to get there. Training books will help you with the various problems you encounter, and it helps to ask the advice of someone who has a good Lab. But don't take the advice of someone who has a poor one!

And remember this, the best hunting dogs are someone's best partners, buddies, pals. As I write this, Lad is lying beside my desk, so close I can reach down and scratch his ears. He sleeps on his own rug beside my bed, he goes to town in my pick-up when it's cool enough, and he goes to the lake with me for a swim or a fishing trip when there isn't a duck with 40 miles. Sometimes he gets half my sandwich in the duck blind, and he likes his coffee with cream and sugar. If you had a Lab that would retrieve 3 ducks at once and could shoot his own limit, I wouldn't trade, and one of these days, when I bury him out there beside old Ram and Freckles and Beau and the other great dogs I've owned, I'll do it by myself, so no one can see the tears.

That bond begins when you take your Lab home as a puppy sitting on the seat beside you with his head on your lap....not inside a crate in the back where his first experience away from the litter has him scared and confused. If that bond developes and he's not always shut up in a kennel, but going places with you and sitting beside you while you read this book and explain it to him....you'll have an easier job ahead of you. I tell folks who come to buy a puppy from me that I can pick the pup which will turn out to be the best dog on the day he is born. It will be the one which gets the most time and attention and love, all other things being the same. If your Lab is a part of your family, you'll lose a lot fewer ducks because of it. And your wife won't worry about you near as much when you go hunting, because she knows she can always trust your Labrador!

51

Dave Meisner relaxes against a flooded pin-oak, watching a flight of mallards.

Chapter 6

Waders

A tree-hugger is a term given to environmentalists at times, but it can also fit those of us who like to hunt ducks. I've done my share of duck hunting from a blind, and I have a portable boat-blind that hides my boat as well as any I have ever seen. But sometimes the best duck hunter is a tree-hugger.

For many years now, Rich Abdoler and I have hunted ducks together, and when we have flooded backwaters, there's no easier way to hunt than to find a pin-oak or a big tree trunk in three or four feet of water to stand against for concealment.

Take for instance that one year just before Christmas when we found ducks along a flat shallow shore next to a lakeside wheat field, and a nearby tree line along a flooded road bed just made for hunters in chest waders. With sunset fast approaching and little time left to hunt, we pitched out a few decoys and found a good tree well out in the water to hide against. In about 30 minutes we dropped two mallards apiece, and decided to return at dawn when there would be more time.

The following morning it was 27 degrees at first light, and we were there in our chest waders, hugging trees in three feet of water along the old road bed. Snow was spitting down from gray skies and the wind was all wrong. But our 40 decoys had drawing power, and in little time, there was a flock of mallards above us, circling, sweeping wide, banking and sailing in on cupped wings only to pull up, circle and return.

Pressed against the tree trunks, covered by branching tangles of dead limbs above us, we were hidden well, and our calls lured the flock in for a final low pass. Shotguns roared and the flock flared away, three of their members folding into the decoys with falling flakes of snow. Minutes later two drakes wheeled behind us and threw caution to the wind, sliding down through the cold gray skies on cupped wings, rocking back and forth with legs down, feet spread. Rich folded one, and I intercepted the other with a load of number three steel.

Forty-five minutes from the time I waded into the water, a squadron of teal rocketed over our decoys and flared above us, and I scored a direct hit on a biscuit-sized drake with my second shot. Shortly after 8:00 a.m., a single drake mallard followed a pair of hens which had landed in the decoys, and the hunt was over, I had my limit of five ducks. I waited while Rich finished his limit within another 30 minutes.

Had we been sitting on that flat with a boat and blind, we would have been lucky to have had a half dozen close, clean shots in a full morning of hunting.

Standing thigh deep in the water, pressed against a tree trunk of which we looked to be a part, we lured ducks into twenty-gauge range, committed to our decoys on set wings. It was a beautiful morning, and a great hunt, simple and uncomplicated, without another hunter within five miles.

Hunting in chest waders isn't always easy.. sometimes the substrate is soft mud, hard to walk through, and sometimes underwater stumps and logs make it necessary to go slowly and with concentration. When you get wet before dawn in 20 degree weather, you have a problem. And your feet get cold without the right layers of stockings and good, lined waders. Still, it's a deadly way to hunt ducks.

I got a letter from one of my newspaper column readers once who said he figured you wouldn't be able to take the cold, standing in the water in a pair of waders. Of course I only use thermally lined waders or heavy neoprene waders which give you the maximum warmth, but I also wear a pair of thermal underwear and or a pair of sweat pants under my hunting pants, depending on how cold it is. In warmer weather, you don't need the sweat pants. Then I use some heavy knee socks over a lighter pair, and pull them well up over my hunting pants so that the hunting pants aren't hiked up as I pull on my waders.

Usually the water temperature of 35 to 40 degrees is warmer than the air so my feet get colder riding in the boat than standing in the water. You need plenty of room in the feet though.... if your wader boots are too small, your feet will suffer.

There's nothing more important to a duck hunter than a good pair of waders, with the exception of course, of a good Labrador. I use a boat with a blind quite often, but given my druthers, when flood waters back up into the timber, I'd druther hunt from a pair of chest waders. When you hunt with waders, you can get away from the crowd by finding a secluded spot where ducks are loafing and feeding, then hide the boat somewhere close by. With decoys bobbing in an open spot, a duck hunter with chest waders can back up against a tree with a limb or two hanging down around him, and occasionally with the use of some camouflage material to hang down around him, be hidden better than he can ever be in a boat. It's a magnificent way to hunt, if you are careful. But don't ever be in a hurry! Waterfowl hunting in chest waders can be hazardous, because there are underwater obstacles, stump holes and yes, the remains of barbed wire fences. You go slowly, or you get wet. It's a horrible feeling to loose your balance in icy water.

I remember hunting in chest waders when the water was only inches from the top of the waders. You learn to move very deliberately at times like that, especially when it's extremely cold. But from time to time, especially in your younger years, you'll get in a hurry wading around out there in deep water, and you'll take a plunge. It has happened to me many times, and to almost everyone I ever hunted with. There's always a stump or a snag down there under

55

the water when you get in a hurry. There are those days when taking a dive is no great problem, other than a little discomfort, but there are those times when getting wet can be extremely dangerous... .on those days when the mercury shrinks to the bottom of the tube.

If you hunt from waders on those kinds of days, be prepared, with a change of clothing perhaps, extra gloves and socks, and some charcoal starter and matches to get a fire going in a hurry. And in cold weather, I like to take along a five gallon metal bucket with six inches of sand in the bottom, and a bag of charcoal, so you can actually have a heater in the boat. You dump some of that charcoal in on top of the sand, soak it and light it, and you have life-saving heat right there in the boat.

Remember too, there's always danger when hunting where there are drop-offs into deep water. If there are creek channels, or holes which might be over your head, or the chance of a sudden drop-off, you can drown in waders because they are so difficult to swim in when they fill with water.

Fifteen years ago, I was hunting in Ontario just off Lake of the Woods. A friend and I were intent on hunting a small beaver pond way in the back of a cove. My partner stepped into a beaver run and went from three feet of water to six or seven feet, and he was really struggling to get out without losing his gun. My Labrador swam past him, and the dog actually pulled him from the depths to solid footing. He said later that as close as the shallower water was, he wasn't sure he could have made it without the Lab to hold onto. The icy water just took his breath, and he had nearly panicked.

Since then, I do not hunt from waders without a float coat. Camouflaged float coats for duck hunters eliminate much of the danger while hunting from waders. If you don't have one, then think of using a ski-belt just above your midsection and below the chest. No matter how much you think you know the area you are hunting, there can always be a hole.

But even with the problems presented by an occasional dip, hunting from waders makes duck-hunting more exciting for other reasons. There's nothing like it for luring ducks in close. Standing against a big flooded oak, I have watched mallards land only fifteen or twenty feet away. And if the water is calm and decoys are sitting stone still, you can ruffle the surface by kicking one foot back and forth, making it appear that ducks are feeding on acorns in the flooded oaks. The decoys don't have to move much, as long as the water is being disturbed. And you can move much more freely with your shotgun, see incoming ducks better and have a far better shot selection than you can from a blind.

Waders allow you to hunt late-season ducks which are very wary of duck blinds. Years ago in early January we were hunting just off the Arkansas river in flooded crop fields where the water was only a few inches deep. Ducks were wanting to light in the very middle of the field, where there was absolutely no cover. We sat down out there in our chest waders, and draped camouflaged burlap over us. Again, the water was only inches from the top of the waders, but the hunting was great. So you don't always have to have flooded timber when hunting from waders. We very often use them to sit on wet, marshy ground next to a pothole or in the back of a lake cove, hidden by a hastily constructed minimum amount of cover.

When hunting from chest waders, you should move the boat away from you, and cover it well. Your Labrador won't want to stay with the boat, so you can fix a platform at water level by using a deer hunter's tree-stand. Because the dog can see so well, it's a great way to train a young retriever. Get him in a position behind you or beside you, and in the shadows. But remember that if you want your dog to learn what that platform is all about, you have to teach him to sit on it before the duck season. A friend of mine taught his Labrador to patiently sit in that tree stand and wait by clamping it to a tree in his front yard, then throwing dummies for him. Little by little he raised the stand until it was better than three feet above the ground. His Labrador began to jump up on the platform on command. Before the season began, he took it to the lake, found a dead tree out in the water to attach it to, and taught his dog to use it. If you intend to wade-hunt in cold water or water of any depth, you need to teach your Lab to use the tree platform before the season begins.

But the bottom line when wading and hunting from chest waders is safety. Go deliberately and cautiously, and wear a float coat. And figure that sooner or later, you are going to get wet. Be prepared for it. And be prepared for some great duck-hunting!

It was a day to remember...when the worst blind in the marsh redeemed itself.

Chapter 7

Old F-13

Some days the wind slings cold rain through the cracks in the blind, and some days the sun is so warm it puts you to sleep as you wait for the mallards that never come.

Some days I ask myself why I hunt waterfowl. For every minute of whistling wings over decoys there are hours of empty skies. Then there are times when it all goes perfectly, the flock that glides in over the tree tops, rocking gently on set wings with landing gear down... an old hen talking to the decoys bobbing in the wind below. The double barrel comes up, two green-heads fold and hurtle to the water. Then your Lab is beside himself with excitement as he charges into the cold pot hole. Moments later both mallards lie at your feet, and the best retriever in the world sits proudly awaiting your praise.

Those are the times that make duck hunting worth any price. And I've enjoyed my share of such moments. But fellow hunters, I have paid the price.

If there's a hunter anywhere who can't relate to bluebird days, dozing in the blind, and a promising young dog that just needs a year or so of hunting to make him the very best . . . well I haven't met him.

We have those days when high hopes vanish early, and those treasured days when everything comes together to create memories that last a lifetime. As the years go by, waterfowlers tend to forget the bluebird days and remember the occasions when great flocks, driven by northern winds, drop into the decoys with the sleet and snow.

There are many such days I like to remember when anticipation of the upcoming season runs high. One of those is a trip I felt sure would be a bust from the beginning. It involved a day in ol' F-13. Now, that would mean little to most folks... but F-13 is a blind at the Schell Osage Public Hunting Area in western Missouri. Some believe that public hunting areas are poor hunting at best. But Missouri waterfowl areas, a half dozen or so of them scattered around the state, have been and still are excellent places to hunt, well-managed and attractive to hundreds of thousands of waterfowl fleeing the advance of winter.

These areas were once hunted by reservation only. Back then you had to apply for a reservation in August and hunt the date for which your name was drawn. But on occasion hunters would cancel their reservations and guys like me could call in and pick them up, as the rules allowed.

The blinds were already built, decoys could be rented, and the hunting was often great. Schell-Osage, one and a half hour north of Springfield, Missouri, is a beautiful marsh, with some excellent blinds, 28 of them in all. There should have been only 27, because ol' F-13 is a bummer.

That blind sits way off by itself, the hardest one to get to, the longest distance from the headquarters, surrounded by trees, facing a little pot hole just off the Osage River. That's bad, because the rest of the hunting area is an open expanse of marsh and abundant water.

Hunters draw for blinds at the area headquarters a good two hours before first light. The place is filled with hunters, and I always wonder what poor soul will draw F-13.

That morning in mid-November of 1979 it was me. My hunting partner, John Green, threw his cap on the ground, kicked it, kicked a tree and called me several names he usually reserved for my Labrador, Beau. John and I had hunted often together in those days, because we worked together. We were good friends before we started working and hunting together. He owned a golden Labrador, and I owned a golden Labrador, and he too often made an unbearable ass out of himself by taking his dog on hunting trips and bragging about him incessantly. Since I always took ol' Beau, John's dog never was necessary, but he never would listen to reason and he took him anyway.

We had obtained a cancelled reservation, and headed to Schell Osage just before the front. It was cold and windy, sleeting occasionally and promising snow. Everything was in our favor until I drew ol' F-13.

On the wall in the headquarters, there were records kept of previous days' hunts. In F-13 there were three "zero's" and a "one" covering the past four days. A week before, some lucky party had downed three ducks from F-13 but they may have been shovelers for all we knew.

John and I had three dozen decoys, and we rented three dozen more. In public areas you need to set a good spread of decoys, and you have to use the call well. Late in the season it's wise to use your call sparingly. And we would have been better off borrowing some decoys because the self-inflatibles rented by the Missouri Department of Conservation weren't the best. There was always one or two which never inflated completely and they look like some stomped duck looking straight up at the sky. But at a dollar per dozen, you didn't expect much.

As we headed for the marsh to load our gear into M.D.C. boats, an occasional fellow hunter would inquire as to what blind we drew. Then they'd make subdued snickering noises in the dark, and get around to letting us know they'd be in A-6, or C-3, where everyone had limited out each day since late October.

John noted that it is darn hard to like other duck hunters when you are motoring off toward old F-13, heading into the dark marsh at the mercy of a 40-year-old five-horse outboard and a maze of boat lanes that could scarcely be navigated during broad daylight. I could understand his feelings. When you're in F-13, it's not just other duck hunters....you don't like anyone!

It's remarkable that we found our blind with such ease. There were no dog fights in the middle of the boat, we hadn't forgotten a thing, and the motor ran like a charm, though we had to reckon with the fact that there was proably not enough gas to get us back.

Dawn's light found us settled in the blind, peering out across 6 dozen decoys huddled in a pothole. John's lab, Rocky, was outside in the specially-made dog blind. Beau was inside with me. We had agreed that every couple of hours, we would rotate the dogs assuming we could get either of them out of where they were.

Ten minutes after shooting hours, a squadron of green-winged teal buzzed our decoys. We were ready for them, somewhat. Each of us got off a shot at the speedsters, flying in a tight formation, and I can't say for sure if either of us dropped a bird. Two went down, and we both speculated that the other had scored a double.

Had it been late in the evening at the close of a poor day, John and I would probably have fought over those two green-wings. But with a whole day ahead, neither of us

Blinds on Missouri's public areas sometimes need attention from each new group to hunt.

64

wanted to claim both ducks, so we each got one. Beau flawlessly retrieved mine, and Rocky managed to stumble across the other and get it back to John.

It wasn't much, but two teal was better production than ol' F-13 had been noted for and it lifted our spirits. Then we sat in that blind for three more hours with very little to do except yell at John's dog, which occasionally wandered away from the blind in search of something to do.

The wind was strong, and it picked up as the morning went on. The gray skies around Schell Osage, normally filled with waterfowl, held little but occasional flurries of snow and sleet. I noticed that there were few shots echoing across the marsh.

Finally, about nine or ten that morning a half dozen mallards came shooting over the tree tops before us, and swung past in a wide circle. There was little chance, I knew. After all, this was F-13. But I had the call, so why not use it.

Less than a minute later, the mallards were hovering over our decoys. The the air was filled with shotgun hulls, ducks fighting for altitude, enthused Labradors and excuses. When the back-slapping was over, it dawned on us that we had three greenheads and two teal, maybe a new record for ol' F-13. But there was no indication we'd see another duck that day. The skies were again empty.

Just before noon, high flights of mallards began to appear, and with some pleading on the duck call, we talked down about 40. Those mallards were intent upon getting out of the wind, and they came in without much discussion. I dropped my third mallard, and John dumped two, making both of us one away from a limit. It was something just short of a miracle. We took some time out for lunch, but gave it up when the ducks continued to fly.

Finally the lack of sleep caught up with John, and he dozed off in his end of the blind. Beau was in the dog blind, anxious for his opportunity to make a retrieve unhindered by non-union labor, namely Rocky.

When a flock of twenty mallards dipped over the tree tops, I saw my opportunity to fill my limit and have some fun out of ol' John, who continued to snore despite the feeding chuckle I sent forth. Calling wasn't really necessary. In only a few seconds, the flock circled, heading into the wind, and dropping in on the first pass. It was too perfect. With John asleep, I emptied my gun at one old drake who just flew away. Beau walked around to the front of the blind to see who had been doing the shooting, then returned to his hideout.

John was awake, and all of a sudden it wasn't such a good joke. There I stood with an empty gun, and the same number of mallards that had swept across the tree tops a minute before were leaving for Arkansas via a strong north wind.

John limited out thirty minutes later on a lone drake that any ten year old kid could have got, and it made little difference that the shot I had taken earlier was affected by the wind, the bottom line was he had his and I didn't. And he crowed about it for an hour.

Determined to get that one last mallard, I waited. With shooting hours ending in only thirty minutes, I worked in a small group of mallards. While John snapped photos, I dropped the eighth greenhead of the day with only one shot.

It didn't exactly make up for the misses. As we gathered decoys, John expounded on the fact that I had greedily allowed a flock of mallards to drop into the decoys without waking him up. It was justice, he said, that I hadn't pulled feather.

I tried to make it up to John. I gritted my teeth and tried my best to brag about old Rocky. With darkness setting in, the old motor died just a hundred yards short of landing, and we had to oar the rest of the way. We pulled into headquarters just as they were about to close up... and our eight greenheads and two teal made up most of all the ducks taken at Schell Osage that day. The strong wind had kept the ducks off the marsh, and hunting had been poor.

Since we were so late, the fellows in A-6 and C-3 were long gone, so there was little bragging to be done, and to this day the guy who checked our ducks thinks we brought them with us.

But that doesn't really matter. What matters is, the mallards were there, my calling was great, and Ol' Beau retrieved like a champion. All right, so maybe I'm not the world's best shot.

As we headed for home, I felt especially generous. "John," I said, "Ol' Rocky done a fine job today.... one of these days he's gonna be nearly as good as Ol' Beau."

For some reason John took offense at that. As my pick-up headed south on the highway, he had to get into a tirade about how I had shot into a whole flock while he was asleep. Geesh, what a poor sport!

Chapter 8

A Little History

The heyday of the market hunter must have been something to see. With black powder, number three shot and double barrel shotguns as large as six and eight gauge, the early duck hunters were efficient. Some of them boasted of taking as many as 3,000 ducks during the fall, and nearly as many again during the return spring flight. In eastern Arkansas, over 100,000 ducks came from one tract of flooded rice in one season. Those ducks were sold, to fancy restaurants back east, to meat markets in the big cities, to anyone who had a taste for wild duck.

The period between 1880 into the early 1900's was the best of times for a man who made his living as a waterfowl hunter. His biggest enemies were the conservationists, men who hunted for sport rather than money. It was they who began to talk of waterfowl depletion, and the eventual extinction of certain species of migratory birds. And lawmakers began to listen. The death of the last passenger pigeon in 1914 gave some urgency to all that.

But it began much sooner, with an organized opposition to spring hunting. By 1900, a handful of northern states had outlawed hunting ducks on their return flights. In May of 1900, the first step was taken toward ending market hunting. It was called the Lacey Act, and it gave the Federal Government control of interstate shipments of waterfowl. And it was the beginning.

In 1913, congress passed the Weeks-McLean Law, which became known as the Migratory Bird Law. And a small organization known as the American Game Protective Association began to grow and gain strength, finding strong allies in two outdoor magazines of the time, Field and Stream and Forest and Stream, the latter being established in 1893 by the Audubon Society.

On the governing board of Forest and Stream was a Senator by the name of George Shiras III who was the primary force behind the passing of the Weeks-McLean Law. That legislation placed all migratory birds under the jurisdiction of the Federal Government. But that law was ignored by many states, with the greatest opposition coming from the south, and from California. One southern legislator lawyer announced that he would defend free of charge anyone arrested for a violation of the law. In Arkansas in 1915, a Federal Judge by the name of Trieber declared the law unconstitutional and released a man who had killed a large number of ducks out of season.

Forest and Stream magazine printed the following comments shortly afterwards on their editorial page:

"When the leaders in the Migratory Bird Law were seeking aid to have this law passed, they did not solicit the help of Arkansas or Louisiana market hunters, but they did appeal to the sportsmen who had been instrumental in having game laws put on the books in states of the middle west. It is hard to get a good game law on the statute books, but the work is nothing as compared with trying to enforce that law. The facts are that the hunters of the middle west will stop shooting if compelled by law to do so, but they fail to understand why it such an unpardonable sin for a sportsman in Nebraska and 25 other states to kill a few ducks when the Federal authorities permit wholesale slaughter in the southern states by market hunters."

"The most ridiculous phase of the situation is that many people and particularly those who wish to break the law—regard the migratory bird law unconstitutional because some ambitious village Dogberry in Arkansas said so in turning loose a man who had shot a few birds out of season. Somebody has started the idea that because this Arkansas judge has overridden by means of his own mind, the dictates of Congress and of the President, then the

Migratory Bird Act must be suspended in operation and ergo everybody is to have a chance to slaughter ducks this coming spring law or no law."

Proponents of waterfowl and migratory bird protection went to President Wilson for help, seeking a way to estab-

lish a solid enforceable set of laws. On July 3, 1918, a special treaty between the U.S. and Canada became law, and it was known as the Migratory Bird Treaty Act. That Act set up federal guidelines controlling the bag limits and limiting seasons on migratory birds. Some southern states revolted against it, Arkansas, Louisiana and Mississippi in particular. Those states were the last stronghold of large scale illegal market hunting. They didn't take kindly to the federal government imposing a limit of three and a half months of waterfowl hunting. Arkansas and Louisiana argued that in the fall, they often had very little water, and the elimination of spring shooting took away the opportunity to hunt when water conditions were best, in the spring.

The Migratory Bird Treaty Act limited hunters to 25 ducks and 8 geese per day. From Missouri, Kansas and Kentucky northward, the season began on September 16 and closed December 31. In Utah, western Oregon, Washington and Connecticut, the season ran from October 1, through January 1. In Texas, Oklahoma, Arizona, New Mexico and California, the season was October 16 through January 31. From Arkansas and Louisiana eastward including Tennessee, Virginia Maryland and all states to the south, the season was November 1 through January 31.

No one knows why the southern states were allowed only a three month season while the rest of the country was given a three and one-half month season. Speculation is that authorities felt the south was the region where state laws were fewer and enforcement harder to gain, and the area where waterfowl was taking the greatest pressure.

But the Migratory Bird Treaty Act would find plenty of opposition elsewhere. In September of 1918, the San Diego Union newspaper printed the following editorial:

"The duck season is about to open. It will be an excellent opportunity to help win the war by killing all the ducks that fly from Tia Juana to Juneau. The wild birds are very destructive to the food crops of this country but as yet we haven't heard the Fish and Game Commissions are doing anything to save the crops. As for the ducks, they should be outlawed year round. Let us turn the market hunter and the pot hunter loose on them."

In January of 1919, amendments were added to the Act, basically beginning what is known as today's two-day possession limits, making it illegal to transport more than two day's limit during any one calendar week of the federal season. Slowly but surely, the Migratory Bird Treaty Act gained the strength and respect necessary to be the salvation of waterfowl. And it happened just in time. Ahead lay the great droughts and dust bowls of the thirties, and the massive drainage projects which destroyed millions of acres of wetlands. But despite the opposition, the ball was rolling.... the majority of the nation's conservationists would eventually overrule those who gave no thought to the future.

History seemed to repeat itself in the 1980's. A controversy developed over lead poisoning in migratory birds and eagles, and steel shot was deemed to be the answer. Again, the greatest opposition came from the south. The first state to adopt steel shot requirements for waterfowl hunters was Nebraska, in 1985. Other states in the north followed with similar laws forbidding the use of lead shot in waterfowl hunting, and eventually, in the mid-'90's even the central provinces of Canada followed suit. Arkansas and Louisiana, and California resisted to the very end, with the Game and Fish Commissions in those states fighting the steel shot requirements vehemently. But by and large the resistance has ended, and as the 21st century begins, the outlook for wild ducks is good. Numbers have been rising in the past few years, and some biologists say there are more ducks today than we have had for the past 50 years. It is a great day for waterfowlers, but we have to work to keep it that way. The vision of those conservationists 100 years ago who started the move to preserve and protect waterfowl must continue with all of us who visit misty morning marshes. In continuing that vision, we now look to the preservation and protection of our wetlands.

Not many hunters welcomed steel shot. It took some time to learn to use it.

Chapter 9

Shooting Steel

"If steel shot regulations are forced upon us, we still may not enforce them; our studies just don't indicate that we have a lead-poisoning problem. Besides, hunters are very much against steel shot, and our responsibility is to the license-holding hunter"

That statement came from the director of the Arkansas Game and Fish commission back in the early '80's. Thank goodness things changed.

After studies in Missouri and Illinois showed hunters that steel shot was, in fact, effective for waterfowl hunting, another study in the state of Louisiana reached the opposite conclusion. In fact, in many of the southern states, such research was often conducted to prove a point already decided upon, in keeping with Murphy's 14th Law, "Enough research will tend to support your own conclusions." Hunters didn't want steel shot anywhere, but they sure as heck didn't want it in the south.

Biologists with the U.S. Fish and Wildlife Service knew back then that lead poisoning was killing waterfowl through lead pellets picked up by feeding ducks and geese. As the problem became more and more severe, steel shot became the only answer.

But one major ammunition company came out of the gate ahead of another in the development of steel shot. The second company, perhaps concerned about financial losses to its competitor, undertook a concentrated effort to discredit steel shot. They promoted the idea that gun barrel damage would result from the use of steel shot and that more crippling would occur. But the main opposition to steel shot came from hunters who were concerned because steel shotshells cost more. And they did indeed cost considerably more. I remember paying sixteen or seventeen dollars per box for three-inch steel shot when it first became required in some of Missouri's public areas. Eventually, a great many of the skeptics were won over, especially as the cost of steel shot began to drop and because significant improvements in steel shotshells were made in a short period of time. The first steel loads weren't very good.. .and a hunter had to learn to lead waterfowl much differently. The bulge in the barrel was a reality in many of the fine double barrels some hunters used, but you could barely see it in all the guns I looked at back then. Experts said there was

no greater amount of crippling with steel shot. But hunters would have to learn that steel shot traveled faster than lead - up to 30 yards or so. At 40 yards, and beyond, it is slower than lead. Therefore, you had to learn to shoot steel shot differently. You didn't lead ducks much at close range, but you needed to lead them a greater amount if they were beyond 35 yards. And it took some learning. None of us came onto it quickly and we all complained. But most of us determined that if it would save waterfowl to hunt with steel, we'd learn to use it. At that time, few hunter knew how to make the necessary adjustments, but little by little we learned.

Since steel shot throws a much tighter pattern, modified and improved barreled guns became the more desirable waterfowl guns. Until then, duck hunters wanted a long-barreled, full-choked shotgun. And if you favored No. 4 lead shot for ducks, you found that No. 2 steel shot was closer to what you were accustomed to. On the other hand, if you've always used No. 6 lead, you wanted to drop down to No. 4's in steel shot. The older you were, the harder it was to adjust, because you had spent so many years learning to lead waterfowl in a certain way, and now you had to learn again. And hunters like my Dad just couldn't accept the idea that short barrels and open chokes could be used to hunt ducks.

The complaint of barrel damage was eventually proven to be unfounded. Studies showed that a slight, nearly imperceptible bulge in the end of the barrel occurred in some of the thin-walled, soft-steel shotguns, but it was seldom very pronounced. My own three-inch magnum Smith and Wesson automatic has fired box after box of steel shot with no evidence of such a bulge or any other damage. Of course, a plastic shot tube within the shell now protects the barrel from contact with the steel.

Overall, the greatest opposition to steel shot came from those who honestly felt that steel shot was less effective in bringing down waterfowl. They argued that steel shot crippled far more ducks, so therefore the number saved from lead poisoning was offset by the number of cripples lost.

Unbiased and reliable studies eventually proved that more cripples did not result from the use of steel shot.

At the same time, authorities suspected that lead poisoning was claiming one to two million ducks and geese each year, and a number of swans and eagles had died from lead poisoning. The eagles were an endangered species, and they got lead poisoning from eating ducks with lead shot in the bodies. There was a great fear at that time that anti-hunting groups would go to court and attempt to end waterfowl hunting because of the lead shot danger to the eagles.

Authorities were betting that as hunters became aware of how serious the lead poisoning problem was, a majority of waterfowl hunters would support the steel shot regulations.

In Ohio in 1981, surveys of hunters showed that those who had used steel shot more than five times, drastically changed their minds about it. Of that group, 33 percent were in favor of steel shot regulations, and 28 percent were opposed, with the remainder undecided. Most of those hunters who had used steel shot only once or not at all opposed steel shot regulations (38 percent against and only 13 percent in favor).

The steel shot situation was put in perspective with the following quote from the Wildlife Society Bulletin, in the spring of 1981, concerning a study conducted by Ohio State University:

"There are many possible reasons for hunters' misconceptions about crippling losses. Szymczak (1 978) reasoned that hunters overestimate crippling losses because they are unable to differentiate between light hits with steel shot and birds severely wounded. Kimball (1974) reported that hunters noted no difference in killing effectiveness or crippling losses when they were unaware of what kind of shot they were using. Anderson and Sanderson (1979) found that two-thirds of the hunters participating in their lead/steel shot tests rated the shells as 'good' whether they had used steel or lead shotshells. When hunters were asked to guess what kind of shells they had used, hunters were more likely to think the lead shells were loaded with steel than to think the steel shells were loaded with lead shot. Hunters' preconceived notions about steel shot undoubtedly stem from the extensive publicity steel shot has received. Roster (1978) mentioned several sources of negative steel shot publicity such as articles in *The American Rifleman*, and *Newsday* magazines."

A federal study conducted at Missouri's Schell-Osage public hunting area in the late 70's proved that there was no significant difference in steel and lead shot crippling rates, nor was there a significant difference in birds bagged per shot. But it would take time to convince hunters who had been misled for years by those who feared they had money to lose with the coming of steel shot. It would have helped if hunters could have seen those ducks killed by eating lead pellets, but few hunters had that opportunity. I found, through my experiences with steel shot, that a hunter could adapt to steel and, in little time, shoot it just as effectively. I missed a lot of ducks learning to use steel shot, but then, I missed a lot with lead when I was learning to use it.

None of us want to live with the thought of fewer ducks and geese year after year because of death by lead poisoning. And waterfowlers have learned that the lead poisoning threat was real. Certainly there are those lightly-hunted wetlands where it isn't ever going to be a problem. But for steel shot regulations and enforcement to work, we all must concede that steel has to be used for waterfowl everywhere with no exceptions.

The advent of Bismuth shot may change waterfowling again, because it is a non-toxic shot which is very close to lead in weight, and is said to perform as the old lead shot loads once did. I haven't used it, and don't know if I will. Steel shot works very well for me now. I don't like the cost of the bismuth shot as this book is being written, but it will likely come down in price in time.

In the meantime, the Department of the Interior has put out a publication entitled "Steel Shot Loads for Waterfowl". They maintain that the best overall shot size for ducks is #3 shot and that #BBB is the best over all shot size for geese. But for situational hunting, they recommend; for large ducks at long range, #1 shot, 1 1/8 ounce load; for large ducks over decoys, #3 or #2 shot, 1 ounce loads; for

The big problem was learning to lead ducks less, or more, depending on the distance.

medium ducks over decoys, #6 to #3 shot, 1 ounce loads; and for small ducks over decoys, #6 to #4 shot, with 1 ounce loads.

My advice is, use heavy loads of #3 or #4 shot to hunt ducks of any size, anywhere, because you usually decoy green-wings, gadwalls, mallards or any other variety of ducks on a single outing. I like to use #2 steel shot on mallards, but it's too large for woodies or teal. High-powered 4's are suitable for mallards too when you don't try to bring down ducks which are out of range. I might use 4's when I know there are mixed species to hunt and many of them are small ducks like teal and widgeon. Given my druthers I'd pick number 3 shot for mallards and bluebills, but that shot size is nearly impossible to find unless you order it. And I would never use 1 ounce loads for any duck hunting except teal hunting....maybe not even for them.

Steel shot cripples ducks when it is used by hunters who aren't knowledgeable about a shotgun's range. I don't like to hunt ducks with 2 3/4 inch shells. I prefer a 3-inch magnum with an improved to modified choke and I want at least 1 and 1/4 ounces of shot when I'm hunting mallards. I think that anyone who hunts ducks with a 20 gauge should do so only if he is very competent with that firearm, and he should always use 3-inch magnum shells. I wouldn't fish for big bass with an ultra-light spinning outfit, and I wouldn't hunt ducks with a 20 gauge.

If you own a 3-inch magnum 12 gauge that is very old, chances are it's a long-barreled full choke gun. You might give some thought to having your barrel shortened, and adding screw-in chokes to make it a more versatile hunting gun. A 30-inch full choke barrel is fine for goose hunting and turkey hunting, but that's a poor duck hunting barrel today.

I had my Smith and Wesson 3-inch magnum automatic, once a full choke 30-inch barrel, cut down to 26-inches and fitted for screw-in chokes. I use three different chokes in it, and I couldn't be happier with the results. Most

81

of the time, when ducks are decoying well, I use an improved cylinder choke with steel shot, but if I'm jump shooting rivers, or hunting late season ducks which are warier, I'm taking longer shots and so I use a modified choke and then maybe go to 1 and 3/8 ounces of shot. Decide for yourself which choke is best by patterning your gun with various chokes at various distances and with different shot sizes.

Duck hunters should be very concerned about the loss of crippled waterfowl....enough so to pass up marginal shots. And if you are a good duck hunter, 90 percent of the mallards you take will be drakes. I make a strong effort to get through each season without shooting a hen. Mallard populations can grow if every hunter will do his part in reducing crippling and passing up hens to take drakes only. If we can do it with pheasants we can do it with mallards as well.

There is a new interest in the 3 and 1/2-inch 12 gauge shot shells and the guns which shoot them. I own one of them, and use it on occasion when goose hunting. But more and more, I stay with 3-inch magnums, because so many times the 3 and 1/2-inch shell is just overkill. Most of the time, I haven't needed the extra power and shot. The loads are punishing, they will brutalize your shoulder and give you a heck of a headache after you shoot a half box or so. But what troubles me most about those guns is the crippling which results when hunters decide they will regularly bring down ducks and geese at 60 and 70 yards. They'll do that some, especially if all you are looking to do is break a wing. But the 3 and 1/2-inch shotguns and even the 10 gauges, are not meant for those kind of shots. If you use those powerful guns, cut down on crippling by learning the range of your shotgun and drawing a line on the distances you shoot.

How lead shot kills ducks

Ingested lead pellets travel to the bird's gizzard along with food. The gizzard then grinds its contents as the first step in digestion. Laboratory tests have shown that a duck is capable of eroding five percent of a pellet in 24 hours, which means that within approximately 20 days a pellet is worn completely away. The eroded lead provides a soluble lead salt that is picked up by the digestive system. This causes severe anemia and drastically limits the blood's ability to provide oxygen and nutrition to the body.

Within several days, the affected bird loses its vigor and eventually cannot fly. Food intake is sharply reduced and the bird begins a downward health spiral that ends in death. Weakened birds seek cover in dense vegetation and, as the lead poisoning process continues, they become extremely emaciated and eventually die in the dense cover or are eaten by predators. Such losses invariably go unnoticed by the public since the weakened birds are adept at hiding. Studies have shown that predators and scavengers can completely eliminate all traces of small-scale losses. Only large-scale losses which occur simultaneously generally are observed, since predators and scavengers cannot remove several hundred to several thousand dead or dying birds concentrated on a few acres.

Chapter 10

As the Wind Blows

The song says they call the wind Mariah. In my duck blind I have called the wind something else at times, always less poetic. If you are a duck hunter, the wind can make you or break you. Hundreds and hundreds of duck hunters have died over the past century because of it, and yet most of the time, a good wind makes duck hunting better. Bluebird days are not so much the days of bright sunshine and warm weather, but those things combined with a complete calm....no wind. I want wind when I hunt ducks.. .and not a warm breeze off the gulf coast, I want to feel cold winds from the Dakotas and the Canadian prairies, a north wind that says snow is in the offing.

But then, come to think of it, late in the season a southern breeze doesn't hurt so much. It something we can tolerate when fall leaves are distant memories and there's ice forming at the edge of the marsh.

You have to remember the wind when selecting a boat and constructing any type of permanent blind on a boat. Its tough to hunt ducks successfully without a boat which you can camouflage quickly, and yet cover miles and miles of open water. A boat with a pre-structured blind is often too slow and sometimes dangerous, especially when whitecaps are rolling. I see these all over the heavily hunted waters, and I can't imagine why. You are placing yourself at a disadvantage when permanent blinds are built on your boat. I hunt big waters from a 17 and 1-2 -foot War Eagle boat powered by a 50 h.p. motor. It takes high waves, and yet, with motor tilted, can be pulled through grassy, shallow waters, so it's great for duck hunters. In stormy weather it can safely haul 3 or 4 hunters, a Labrador, decoys and gear.

85

I don't use a preconstructed blind, because I set up my blind when I get to the place I want to hunt and after decoys are set. It goes up and comes down in a matter of minutes. The secret to this light but effective blind is a strong, lightweight material which doesn't absorb moisture, which has come to be known by a variety of names. The material comes in different colors and patterns, and what I use today is made by a hunter specialties company in Alabama known as "Hide-em-Hunter" company. The first material I used 25 years ago was developed and manufactured by a well known Minnesota waterfowler, Don "the duck man" Helmeke.

"The tradition of duck hunting has a powerful influence on the way we hunt today," he told me in a recent phone conversation, "because years back the outdoor magazines featured articles which emphasized small boats and small blinds."

"The best duck hunters stressed that," he said, "and hunters died in boats that were too small for the waters they hunted. We have materials today which will camouflage a big boat as easily as a small one. It isn't the size of the blind that flares ducks, its other things which hunters can control."

This blind is light and effective and sets up when we get to a hunting spot.

Helmeke is right. If your duck hunting is done on small waters and marshes you can use a small boat to get there and back. I also have one of those boats I hunt from. But a small boat which is unstable can be unsafe to shoot from. Thirty years ago all waterfowling was done on those shallow marshes and rivers. And it was much the same in the north country, except for the bluebill and canvasback hunting on big waters like Lake of the Woods. In the deep south, small boats were used in the flooded timber just to get there and get back. Few hunters actually hunted out of those boats, they got out and stood in the flooded timber in their waders. We didn't have lakes like Truman and Dardanelle and Rathbun and Glen Elder then, but now there are huge impoundments which attract ducks all over the Midwest, in Iowa, Kansas, Oklahoma and Arkansas and Missouri.

So things are different now. You begin to see hunters looking for ducks and geese on big waters, and its necessary to have a boat which can handle the wind and waves. But no matter what boat you use, use your head as well. On lakes like Stockton and some of the eastern Kansas reservoirs where the wind gets a long uninterrupted run at you, whitecaps are high most of the winter. Sometimes its better to make different plans when there is blustery, stormy weather. Don't risk your life in water which you don't have the experience for.

There is danger in duck hunting, and it increases when you are hunting new waters, in regions you aren't familiar with. To illustrate this, let me tell you about a place known as Netley Marsh in Manitoba, which lies at the southern edge of the giant Lake Winnipeg. Lake Winnipeg is about 80 miles wide in places, and about 240 miles long, north to south. Therefore, when a strong north wind blows for a long period of time, it pushes water from the big end of the lake into Netley Marsh which lies at the southern end. This shallow grassy marsh looks safe and harmless when the wind is calm, or out of the south. You can motor out into some of the most beautiful duck habitat you've ever seen, and get out and stand in those reeds much like you would do on small waters and marshes in the Dakotas or Nebraska's sand hills. And when hunters do that, they often just pull their boat into the reeds somewhere and cover it.

Over the past 120 years there's no telling how many hunters have died when the north wind moves water into the marsh, and it slowly rises higher and higher until boats float away and hunters are trapped, at the mercy of the rising waters with no high ground to flee to. The first time I hunted that marsh 15 or 20 years back, a guide who had been there since the 1940's took me aside and explained what could happen. Countless numbers of hunters over the decades lost their lives because they didn't know.

A few years ago, some local hunters had to spend a cold night on Truman Lake when they were capsized by wind and waves trying to return to a nearby boat ramp. They spent most of the night in misery waiting to be rescued, and could have died of hypothermia if it had been later in the season and the temperature colder. Four other hunters in two separate duck hunting incidents that same night at Mark Twain Lake and on the Mississippi River, lost their lives. The story is usually the same... .boats too small, or made top heavy by preconstructed blinds, sometimes overloaded. They too often go out in October conditions, and come back in a December-type blizzard.

I remember a day like that in December of 1983. My old friend Mac Johnson came down to hunt with me on Truman Lake, and we met well before first light at a restaurant at Clinton, Missouri. I remember how I complained about the weather, it had been too nice. Too clear, too calm, too warm, shucks we had been hunting in shirt sleeves. But Mac said there was a blue norther headed our way that would change all that, heavy snow already in the Dakotas and approaching Iowa and Nebraska... ice being reported in western Kansas and plummeting temperatures a certainty by evening.

At the restaurant, we talked to four hunters from the

Kansas City area, and in the parking lot, they had one of those boats with plywood and camouflage and limbs and grass. It was too small for two hunters and all their gear, let alone four. And it was top-heavy with the blind. Then they had a Labrador to add. The leader of the four, who was a big man, looked at my boat and wondered where the blind was. I told him it was packed away to be used if and when I needed it. He told me, before he left, that my boat was too big.

I learned a long time ago that it is of little use to argue with someone about hunting or fishing so I just agreed with him and went on. I didn't tell him that before I'd navigate Truman Lake in the predawn darkness in his boat, I'd hunt the water trap at the local golf course, but I would have.

I can't remember much about the morning hunting that day, so it must not have been very good. Long before noon, Mac and I came in and relaxed awhile and had some dinner. The sun, high and bright, began to sink into a gray cloud cover just after noon and by one or two p.m., the wind was gusting strong out of the northwest, and cold. The temperature was sinking fast. We motored a considerable distance up a tributary, found a small flooded crop field and hid the boat back in the timber beside it. Standing against some big trees at the edge of the field in crotch-deep water, we threw out a dozen decoys and waited. By three or four p.m., ducks started appearing high above us, at first a flock here and there, maybe six or eight at a time. Then way up high, there were flocks of 50 or 60, then groups of 90 or 100 at a time, then several hundred above us at once. They were flight ducks, riding the wind and fleeing the blizzard to the north. They were tired and ready to set in for the evening where there was food and protection from the ever increasing wind. And it was the kind of thing you don't often see, the circumstances hunters dream of. Mallards fell in finally in growing numbers, flock after flock, one group circling at one altitude, another above and still more above them. Eventually it was just a huge throng of mallards descend-

89

ing in a spiral, with almost none of the approaching, picking up and recircling you usually see.

They fell in from great heights, side-slipping and nearly turning over to lose altitude, a sight you live to see if you are a duck hunter. Flocks that were small specks in the high greyness were dropping into the fields and flooded timber like leaves in a great whirlwind. Mac and I had our limits in less than 30 minutes at the first of it, so then we stayed to watch the magnificence of it as the day grew darker and the wind stronger.

Finally we knew we should leave to give the ducks a chance to settle and stay, and we also knew that when we reached the mainlake, we'd be coping with some big-time white-caps.

It was even worse than I expected. The temperature had dropped 30 degrees in a matter of hours, and it was 17 degrees when we got in. I was covered with ice from the spray, and even with my goose down parka, chilled to the bone. That big 18-foot boat had crossed the white-caps, but if the lake had been much wider there we would have left the boat and walked out. I never thought about the men we had talked to after breakfast that morning, I guess I figured they would have gone in much earlier.

But they waited too long, and in that fierce gale, they tried to cross the lake in that small boat with the built-on blind. They didn't make it.

Another good hunting friend, Rich Abdoler, is a Corps of Engineers Ranger on Truman Lake, and he was called out that night to look for the men. The following morning they found scattered decoys and the boat washed up on the shore. Later, the bodies of three of the hunters were found, supported by life jackets, but dead from hypothermia, apparently long before they could reach the shore. In the intense cold, Truman was rapidly freezing over, and though helicopters found the body of the fourth man later in the week, his body could not be recovered from the ice for nearly two months. Only the Labrador survived.

I have learned over the years to not take chances. My boat won't cross every body of water when the whitecaps are high... and I can walk out, or spend the night somewhere if I have to. You can get yourself in a bad situation while hunting ducks without much difficulty because of the cold and the water you'll deal with from time to time. But it is the boat that will cause most of the deaths amongst waterfowlers. Don't overload a boat, don't challenge a wind you can't handle and don't settle for a boat which is too small for the water.

I have a small boat which I use in flooded backwaters and on small streams, but when I'm hunting ducks on one of our reservoirs, I use my 18-foot, 72-inch-beam lake boat, powered by a 60 horse motor. And there's no blind on it until I get to where I intend to hunt. When it's possible, we just hide the boat and cover it, and hunt in chest waders. That's always the best way to hunt ducks, if it's possible. If not, I haul out my portable duck blind and cover the boat with it. It takes less than ten minutes to set it up, and it doesn't weigh fifteen pounds.

But even with that big boat, I won't try to cross any lake if there's wind which represents a threat, and Ozark duck hunters need to take that attitude. If you aren't sure you can make it, don't take the risk. Find a place on shore that's out of the wind, build a big fire and wait it out. If you know the area fairly well, you can probably walk out and return for your gear the next day. No one is going to steal it on a cold, dark, stormy night. There's hardly an area on any of our reservoirs where there's not a road or house within a couple miles.

Be ready for such situation with some good flashlights, and have walking shoes in your boat somewhere if you are hunting in chest waders. And be prepared for the threat of hypothermia by stashing a heavy pair of coveralls and some heavy socks and gloves in plastic bag, just in case someone goes in the water.

For an emergency heat source, I take a metal five gallon bucket with four or five inches of sand in the bottom, with a sack of charcoal and some lighter fluid inside. It sits out of the way until it is needed, and then it gives off a great amount of heat in a small area in a hurry.

Almost every one who hunts ducks can recall a situation on a past hunt which was potentially dangerous. We've all tripped and fell in at one time or another, and faced white-caps that were just too high. If you are a veteran or a beginner, you need to be sure you have the emergency gear along to handle a dangerous situation in the cold. And you need to have the common sense to look at rough water and stay put. There may be some discomfort with sitting around a fire on a cold night waiting for a storm to subside, but the dawn of a new day is worth waiting for. Too many duck hunters don't see it because they take a risk.

If you figure percentages, I'm absolutely sure that more waterfowl hunters have died over the years in accidents than deer hunters. But there's much less danger if you think ahead to include the proper gear for emergencies, and refuse to take risks. Put a kill switch on your motor and use a boat large enough for the job. And don't be caught on an interstate highway riding in a go-cart...hunt in a boat big enough to get you out there and back safely.

Boats

As I said in the first chapter of this book, I grew up hunting ducks out of wooden johnboats which my dad and granddad built. They were usually 14 or 15 feet long, and at the midsection, about 40 inches wide. Those boats were so stable that a grown man could walk down the top side of them and not dip water. We would usually hunt three men to a boat, one paddler and two hunters on the front seat, side by side. It was jump-shooting at it's best, covering ten or twelve miles of the river in one day, sneaking up on mallards and wood ducks and teal with the help of a concealing blind attached to the bow of the boat, made from oak, maple and willow limbs.

About the time I left home to attend college, a boat company from Lebanon, Missouri visited my grandfather and looked at his boats, talking to him at great length about making an aluminum version of those wooden johnboats. That Richline-Appleby boat company eventually made a river boat much like the old wooden johnboats, so easy to handle with a boat paddle that folks quit making their own. Eventually, they became known as the Lowe Boat Company, and the paddle boat was called a "paddle-john". In lengths of 16 to 18 feet, the paddle john was made for 20 years or so, and then dropped in the mid-'90's.

It was not only a great river-floating boat, it was a great small-water duck boat, and I used it, with a small six horse motor, or simply a paddle and no motor at all. We hunted ducks out of those paddle-johns all over the Midwest, in waters where bigger boats were impractical, and in places where you needed to physically carry a boat to the water because of the lack of a road or launching ramp.

We were hunting geese in Manitoba one year when we noticed that geese left the fields about mid-day in the region we hunted and flew into a shallow, marshy lake on private ground, where they loafed and rested with several thousand ducks. Before we left that year, we got permission from the owner to hunt the marsh the following year. But he said we'd have trouble, others had tried to hunt it, but it was boggy, and you just couldn't wade out to where you needed to hunt. There wasn't a good place to unload a boat, and most hunters in that region had big boats with motors. The little marsh was a great place for waterfowl, but for most hunters, just unreachable.

The next fall, we took my little 17-foot paddle -john to Canada with us, and easily slipped it into the shallow marsh, paddling it just where we wanted it, setting decoys and then hiding in the high reeds. I doubt if there had been a hunter there in years. The only problem was, it was just too easy. We had a limit of geese in less than an hour, big Canadas which drifted in no more than 30 yards from our covered, well-hidden boat. We sat in the bottom of it, on a cushion of straw, and picked our shots, with our heads only a couple of feet above the waters surface.

Light but stable boats are worth their weight in gold to a duck hunter who hunts shallow, small waters. But don't even think about hunting ducks from a canoe. I know that people do it, but canoes aren't safe, and they are not made for duck hunting. The exception might be the 18-or 19-foot square-sterns. I've used a 19-foot Grumman square-stern canoe on occasion in shallow marshes, but I wouldn't even think about hunting from one of those double-end canoes,

94

the capsize-and-chaos specials that everyone uses when the weather is warm and the water feels good when you get dumped. Well-built square-sterned canoes have some stability, but the johnboats have more if you stay away from the short ones which can sometimes be tipsy.

For big waters, I used an 18-foot aluminum boat for many years also made by the Lowe company with a six-foot

Mike Dodson with geese shot from a small paddle boat in a secluded Manitoba marsh.

beam and no bench seats between the front and back decks. Duck hunters don't want bench seats in bigger boats, because you need to walk from front to back, and they just get in the way when you have a blind on your boat.

I have always used my boat for both hunting and fishing. In fact, I have taken it to Canada for both purposes,

The War Eagle duck boat.

hunting ducks in the morning, and fishing in the afternoon. An attached front deck with trolling motor and pedestal seat could be added or removed with an electric screw-driver.

In the mid-90's an old boat company took a new direction, and began building duck hunting boats which could double as fishing boats. The boats come in all sizes, one of them being the 18-foot, 72-inch-beam, lake boat like those which I have so long used, easily converted to a fishing boat with trolling motor and fishing pedestal seats.

The old company was a big name in midwestern boats, the Dura-craft Boat Company in Monticello, Arkansas. John Ward and his brothers were grandsons of the man who started that company back in the 1950's. They now own and operate the War Eagle boat company in Monticello, and there are few avid duck hunters who don't know about those boats. They are unique in many ways, the camouflage paint job, the non-slip camouflaged floor covering and a T-rail around the boat which allows for adding all kinds of options just by attaching them to that rail. Options include a step platform for Labradors, and a deep-water step to enable hunters to climb into the boat from waist deep water.

There are other addables, a grip to hold the boat solidly against tree trunks, a sealed beam headlight, gun holders, duck blinds, etc. But the idea is to get away from what other boat companies are doing....just building boats of a certain size and type. The Ward brothers try to build a boat as close as possible to the specifications of an individual buyer. And a percentage of each boat they sell goes to Ducks Unlimited.

I'm sure there are other companies making duck boats, specifically designed to hunt from, and to use with duck blinds, and that's something new. It's a great time to be a duck hunter, with increasing numbers of ducks, better gear and warmer clothes, and better boats. But think about it...use a boat that is completely safe for the water you hunt and the way you hunt.

Jim Killer was an accomplished duck hunter before he was out of college.

Chapter 11

Hunting With a Jonah

Over the years I've hunted ducks with a good number of people, and my best friends today are men I got to know in some swamp or marsh. Men with scraggly beards and patched waders are most often men of sterling character. Find a man who treasures an old beat up pump gun and extols the virtues of a Labrador retriever and you've found a man of substance. Usually!

There have been exceptions. Many years ago I had three good friends who were wildlife management students from Arkansas Tech University at Russellville, Arkansas. We all worked together, and duck hunting helped make us even closer friends.

Jim Killer worked for the Fish and Wildlife Service for a time and then got into advertising. John Green worked as a state park superintendent for many years before opening his own business, and Mike Widner is now the wild turkey biologist for the Arkansas Game and Fish Commission.

All three knew a great deal about the Arkansas River Valley of western Arkansas, and where to find the best duck hunting. Jim and Mike were two of the finest duck callers I've ever hunted with. John and I were learning from them. Men of substance, I thought, until that day in December of 1973.

We had hunted an especially good spot that morning a few miles from Dardanelle, Arkansas, and as I remember it, I made some extra good shots. It was one of those occasions when all the opportunities came my way and I made the most of it. I wouldn't say I bragged about it, I merely pointed out that my friends had fired more rounds for less ducks than I had. We stopped in a small Dardanelle restaurant for a bite to eat, and my lack of sleep caught up with me. We had set forth just after 4:00 a.m. and if I'm not mistaken most of the night before had been spent recalling and stretching duck hunts of years past.

I got to bed about two a.m., so by late morning the next day, I was extraordinarily exhausted. I sat down in a booth beneath a warm heat vent, ate a hamburger and waited for my friends to finish theirs. I leaned my head against the wall, and it knocked my old duck hunting cap askew, but I didn't notice, because I dozed off just a little. In fact I fell into such a deep slumber my mouth fell open just a bit and my cap nearly fell off. My three good hunting buddies got up and quietly sneaked out, noting that two Dardanelle policemen were pulling into the parking lot.

As if it weren't bad enough to leave a friend asleep in a deep corner of a fast food joint, they made it a point to direct the policemen my way, insisting I was either inebriated or dead or both. Because I am somewhat addled when suddenly awakened, I wound up reciting the whole alphabet while trying to explain I was only a duck hunter, without any decent friends. Over the years, I forgave them, and we hunted ducks together in many different wetlands of the Midwest.

Mike Widner and I once hunted ducks in southern Iowa on one-day with a reservation at Missouri's Fountain Grove waterfowl area the next morning. The rules at that public area say you have to be at the area headquarters at four a.m., so we left Iowa just

after dark and arrived at Fountain Grove late that night. Signs directed us to a small campground not far from the headquarters and we set up a tent rather quickly in total darkness. About 3:30 a.m. we were awakened from a sound sleep to learn that we had erected that tent only fifteen feet from a railroad. Mike and I circled the inside of the tent several times as the train bore down upon us and roared past, but we never found the zipper that opened the door, thank heavens. Neither of us have ever slept so little and yet been so awake as we were at dawn that morning. But we didn't shoot well for most of the morning. The gun barrels were shaky.

The following year John Green and I had another duck hunting reservation at Fountain Grove early in the duck season. We were fishing in southern Wisconsin the day before and as usual, we got a late start toward northern Missouri, figuring on driving all night and taking turns sleeping. It led to one of the most awkward situations I've ever been involved in while hunting waterfowl.

We had purchased a dozen decoys which had no anchor weights, and we decided that temporarily, we could perhaps use some old spark plugs or discarded lead weights used to balance tires.

So about two o'clock in the morning we happened across an all-night service station just outside a small northern Missouri town. Surely there'd be something we could beg or borrow to use for anchors.

The lone attendant cast a sleepy but suspicious eye toward our pickup, where the barrel end of a pair of shotgun cases were sticking up in plain view.

"Uh...sir I was, uh.... well uh," I said. "We were wondering if," .... the guy really looked uneasy as I searched for the right words. "Geez, I hate to bother you for this," I went on, "but we need some used spark plugs for our ducks."

I didn't mean ducks of course, I meant decoys, but it was late and I had been asleep. I noticed then that this guy was edging toward his desk looking panicky and I started wondering if he had a gun in there. So I started getting panicky too.

"Oh I don't mean ducks," I said, trying to sound relaxed, hoping he'd know that relaxed people don't rob filling stations. "Well we don't have real ducks, ours are rubber." I said searching frantically for the right words.

"You see we bought some today," I went on, "and we've already got enough string for them, but... well no they're not really rubber ducks, they're uh..."

Finally John decided to help out. "Decoys!" he yelled from the pickup, "Decoys!"

It was too late. The attendant had bolted for the office and slammed the door behind him. I headed for the pick-up on a dead run and John had it rolling before I got in. We finally came up with some weights for the decoys that night, but a lot of good it did us. We spent most of the next day asleep in the blind.

We never got much sleep back in those days.. there just wasn't much time. Duck hunting took all of the day-light hours when we weren't working. One Friday afternoon Mike Widner got off work early and headed for the marsh in his old beat up pick-up. The place we were hunting back then had some old roads going in there, but they were in bad shape and some of the mudholes were so deep you could nearly hunt them. But Mike would get a good run at them and get through, then unload his boat in a small creek and paddle a half mile to a little pothole he liked to hunt. Mike hunted alone that Friday evening and didn't quit 'til the last minute ticked off the clock. By the time he picked up the decoys and loaded his boat in the back of the pick-up, it was well after dark.

His old pump gun had seen it's better days and Mike never worried too much about taking care of it. It was an old off-brand twelve-gauge he had bought from somebody for 20 dollars and the truth is, he didn't take real good care of the gun. If it shot and ejected shells, Mike was happy. And after all, it killed ducks over decoys just as well as a new Browning. That evening Mike made a mistake in his haste and left the gun on the tailgate beside the boat. When he got back home, he had everything but the gun...but Mike didn't worry. He knew what had happened, and he knew where the shotgun had to be. The old pick-up had bucked it out at that first mudhole.

John Green joined him before daylight the next morn-ing and the only account of what happened is the story

John tells 'til this day. He said Mike put on his waders, drove through all the bad places until he got to that one mudhole, turned off the keys and got out with only his headlights to see by. John said Mike hadn't even hinted he was missing his shotgun, but he mumbled something about finding it, and waded out into that mudhole, feeling around with his boots in knee-deep water.

Mike Widner with his old pump gun...sometime after the mudhole incident.

John watched in amazement as his hunting buddy reached down into the water past his elbows and came up with that shotgun, turning the barrel down to drain the water, and looking it over in the dim light of the headlights. Then he got in, asked John to hold the gun and he hit that mudhole about 30 miles per hour.

John said that they killed a limit of ducks that morning, and Mike's gun performed as it always did, with very few misses. Loaded up, Mike told John to remind him to clean his old shotgun good when he got home, and they hit that mudhole again. That last time, the boat came out. But at least, as they both recall, it floated!

That year John and Mike and I got our first Labradors... three yellow pups from the same litter which were about six months old when the season opened. We were trying to convince Jim Killer that he needed to get a retriever too. Hunting together at the Schell-Osage waterfowl area, John and Jim and I worked a flock of mallards and dropped two or three. Our Labrador pups were excited about it all, but short on experience. They followed us out into the water as John and I retrieved the ducks, and Jim watched.

Back in front of the blind we tossed the dead mallards out into the decoys and our pups retrieved them with enthusiasm. After watching two or three such retrieves, Jim remarked that he was impressed. "All you fellows have to do is go get your ducks the first time, he grinned, "and those dogs will get 'em from then on." Eventually Jim acquired a Labrador too, and we went from arguing about who could outshoot whom to who had the best retriever.

I gained new duck hunting friends as the years passed and I became a full-time outdoor writer and photographer. Dave Meisner was the publisher and editor of Gun Dog magazine until he sold it in 1985. From Adel, Iowa, Dave was a top flight upland bird hunter and a man who loved hunting dogs. I volunteered to teach him the fine art of duck hunting. Dave had two friends from Des Moines, Norm and

Rob Beattie, brothers who operated a business together. The four of us hunted together during much of the 1980's and had some great times, but it can now be said that Rob Beattie was a genuine Jonah.

A Jonah of course is a man besieged by bad luck. Norm and Dave knew it from the beginning I think, because they so often left poor ol' Rob floundering around in the marsh on his own. I found out about Rob's dark cloud of bad luck during a 1986 hunt in the sandhills of northeast Nebraska. The week before, Rob had gone to a Duck's Unlimited banquet and bid on what he thought to be an expensive foreign shotgun, or so I theorize. But the German Draathar turned out to be a weird looking puppy, and Rob turned out to be the only bidder. So there he was in Nebraska with one of the ugliest six-month-old hunting dogs I've ever seen.

Nebraska's sandhill waterfowl hunting is sensational during those wet years when ranch lakes are full. These small natural lakes are surrounded by high reeds and grasses, and they are used by nesting mallards, teal, gadwall, ringnecks, redheads, and other species.

It is sparsely settled country, without many duck hunters. In fact the first time I went there I was hunting prairie chickens and sharptail grouse. But I became acquainted with several ranchers who invited me back to hunt waterfowl, and I found duck hunting that was outstanding, with no competition.

When Rob and I arrived, it had been raining about an hour, and it continued for most of the three days we were there.

We rented a motel room in a small Nebraska town and drove toward the ranch where we were to hunt, well before daylight. There were about 18 miles of narrow, wet sand roads ahead of us, and we slid all over them. To make matters worse, my two-year-old Labrador and Rob's hyper, whiskered pup were confined in the area behind the seat of my super-cab pickup. Ram didn't like foreign dogs and the pup wanted to play.

Rob had been trying to kick the smoking habit, but between the dog-fight behind us and the soggy sand roads before us, he smoked an average of three cigarettes per mile. Finally the road played out early, about four miles short of the ranch, where recent grader and dozer work made it too soft to go farther. With shooting hours 30 minutes or so away, I stopped at the ranch house we had just passed to ask if there was another way to get where we were going.

The old rancher we talked with was one of the nicest people I've ever happened across. He said we didn't have to worry, he had a 20-acre lake that was full of ducks which hadn't been hunted in years, and we could drive right to it.

It's hard to explain this, but when the sandhills are soaking wet, it's easy to drive almost anywhere except on the roads. We had no trouble getting in to the prettiest little lake you'd ever want to see. We slipped my square-sterned Grumman into the water, loaded some decoys and paddled into a nice little bay bordered by high reeds, flushing several hundred ducks in the process.

Things really began to look good. The dogs settled down a bit and the rain slackened some. My raingear apparently had no leaks and my chest waders were brand new. It wasn't real cold, and ducks were flying.

We weren't ready at shooting hours, but we situated our boat back into the reeds at about the time we would have seen the sunrise if it hadn't been raining. The decoys bobbed invitingly as I loaded my shotgun, and I remember telling Rob that things were really looking up. After all we had been really lucky to find such a great spot, and we hadn't slid off in the ditch, and if his pup turned the boat over, the water wasn't more than waist deep.

Maybe Rob wasn't really a Jonah, I thought, as the realization hit me that his pup was even uglier when wet. That's when the first flock of ringnecks rocketed across our decoys. My shotgun bucked once against my shoulder and one duck hurtled stone dead into the rain-pocked lake. Poor

Rob didn't even get off a shot. But his pup was out there swimming around behind ol' Ram, who was retrieving the prettiest 100 point redhead drake you'll ever want to see. I had limited out with my first shot!

Rob was, after all, a Jonah. Pulling my boat from the water at 10:30 a.m. I ripped my waders on a hidden strand of old rusty barbed wire, and it began to rain even harder, with an ominous streak of lightning across the western sky.

Apparently Rob's luck never did get any better, because I talked to Norm Beattie awhile back and he said Rob still has that dog! Once a Jonah, always a Jonah.

A genuine Jonah...but a great guy. Rob Beattie and his Draathar pup.

The author with "Brown-eyed Beau," back in the good old days.

Chapter 12

Ducks In the Good Old Days

Several years ago a beginning waterfowler joined me and a friend in our duck blind. The ducks weren't decoying well; in fact, they were just passing by on their way south, flying way up there at the edge of the ionosphere as if a blizzard was blowing at their heels. My partner and I were having some fun with the greener who had finagled his way into this hunt by marrying into my partner's family.

"Look at that bunch," I said as a group of ducks flew over so high I doubt they'd show up on radar. "Redheads!"

My partner decided to spread it a little deeper. "Yeah, but would you look at that. There's a canvasback up there towards the front." Then he switched his gaze to another small V formation coming over to the right, and said, "And there's a flock of mallards."

Squinting, I counted the ducks and agreed. "Yup, four hens and seven drakes." The beginner between us shook his head and murmured something about how we really knew our ducks. I winked at my partner. Maybe later we'd try to sell this guy a life-time membership to this public hunting area.

Watching the high-flying ducks, I heard the poor guy wishing they'd fly just a little bit lower. Going along with the idea that the grapes which cannot be reached are considered sour, I commented that almost all those high flyers were redheads, one hundred point ducks in those days. My partner explained that no true sportsman would shoot a redhead or canvasback, and I indignantly remarked that I was ashamed to be sitting in a blind with someone who even wished he could get a shot at one.

Things went from bad to worse, and an hour later we veterans were asleep, caps pulled down over our eyes, guns leaning in the corners of the blind. In the middle, that would-be hunter sat staring at the decoys and hoping.

I guess it was the whisper of wings that woke me up. As I reached for my gun, I noticed the beginner standing up pointing his automatic at the flock. By the time I got to my feet, a flock of 30 or 40 pintails were just out of range, and he hadn't fired a shot.

As we watched them fly away, my partner straightened his hat and asked his in-law why the greenhorn hadn't shot.

"I almost did," he said, sighing, "but I think they were some more of those darned redheads."

My hunting friend and I get together every now and then and laugh about that. He says that relative of his moved to another state and became a veteran waterfowler. I can't remember at all if we got any ducks that day.

And that's something to remember... .some of the greatest waterfowling memories I have, rise from the ashes of trips that didn't produce any startling results. Of course, I've got some memories from good hunts too. There was a time, several years back, when some friends and I made a December duck hunt in an Arkansas public hunting area. We were standing out in some flooded pin oaks at dawn, and the ducks were really flying. One of the guys casually mentioned that he hoped I had my duck stamp, knowing how forgetful I was. I told him that my federal stamp (Arkansas had no state stamp then) was firmly attached to my Missouri non-resident license since I had been hunting up there in October. And I had my Arkansas hunting license too, since I had bought both back in January.

My partner knew I had lived in Arkansas only a year. He shook his head and said, "Brother! I'm bettin' you don't have a valid hunting license. Remember, in Arkansas the license is good from July 1 to June 30."

I hastily dug out my license, and there it said in small, not-so-bold letters, that my license purchased in January of 1974 had expired in July 1974.

So I left the shotgun in the limbs of an oak, and waded out to find a license while I listened to my buddies shoot ducks. In the parking lot, next to my pickup, sat a conservation agent in his pickup, sound asleep.

When I returned an hour later with my new license, the agent was still there, still asleep. I waded back out to find my friends waiting with their limits of mallards. They waited and watched as I limited out in the next hour, and I had the last laugh. And I swear, when we loaded up and left the marsh just before noon, that same game warden was sitting in the parking lot, still asleep in his pick-up.

I remember the time back then when an old friend of mine drove down from Missouri, to try some of Arkansas' hunting. Mac Johnson, who was the editor of the Missouri Conservation Department magazine, "The Conservationist", eventually convinced us all that a Labrador is worth more to a duck hunter than anything else he owns. But Mac came to Arkansas on the heels of a cold snap, and all of our favorite spots were frozen over. I introduced him to my new duck hunting companions, Jim Killer and Mike Widner, who knew that country like a bear knows bees. Jim said he knew of a great spot under such conditions, a big sand bar on the Arkansas River just up from the mouth of the Petit Jean River.

He and Mac built a blind there on that sand bar, but we agreed it would be hard to hide four hunters and a dog, so Mike Widner and I headed up the Arkansas river in Mike's boat, looking for a good place to build a blind. We passed up a couple of good spots, finally settling on a perfect sand bar where a big log and root-wad would help hide us.

We knew all about the Federal refuge on the Arkansas River known as Holla Bend, but we thought we were miles away. After all, there were no signs to suggest otherwise, and we felt certain the refuge boundary would be marked.

Mike and I fired a few rounds, made some excuses, and

killed a couple of mallards. When I retrieved the last one from our decoys, I noticed a man walking down the sandbar toward us. An agent, I correctly assumed, about to make a routine check of a couple of good sportsmen who wouldn't break the law for anything.

Ignorance of the law is no excuse, but when it's the only one you have, well, you grasp at straws. And we darn well were ignorant as to where we were. According to the agent, the Holla Bend Refuge boundary ran through our makeshift blind and through the decoys. True, there were no signs, since the river would wash them away.

Mike Widner was a great hunting partner...partly because he could call ducks with the best of them.

The Federal Agent was a nice guy, but we were dead wrong and there wasn't much use in begging for mercy. I did anyway — on my knees, I think. The agent said if we could get all our gear in the boat, load the decoys, and get downriver to the next sandbar before he changed his mind, he'd let us go with a warning. He said he knew I had indeed acted out of ignorance, because he had read some of my articles. I still don't know how he meant that, but we were heading down the Arkansas before he could have changed his socks, if not his mind. All that was left to indicate what a monumental goof we had made were a few cane sprigs, and my knee-prints in the sand.

Mac's yellow Labrador really impressed us back then. Her name was Gypsy, and she was smart. Mac said he ate lots of apples when he hunted ducks, and he always gave Gypsy the apple cores, which she loved. But he swore that on his last trip she had rummaged into his lunch while he napped, took out an apple and ate all of it but the core. She left that core on the bench beside him as if to say, "You try the core for once!"

When Gypsy had puppies, Mike and Jim and I each bought one. I was only about 23 then, and old Beau was my first Labrador. I've never been without one since and never will be. As is often the case with close friends, Mac gave us the pups at a fraction of their value; he even told me I could make monthly payments over the next two years at 25% interest. But I got even with him. Several years later I called Mac and told him I was itching to float the Big Piney River in southern Missouri. I grew up on the Piney, and I loved to float the river in the fall with a blind on a john-boat, jump shooting ducks.

I told Mac on the phone that I was sure there'd be ducks all over the river retreating before the front. If he'd drive down to the Piney, I'd meet him there and we would knock off two limits with little or no effort.

Poor Mac left well before dawn, drove for two hours and got to the Piney about an hour before I did. We got started

Mac Johnson and a young Labrador.

about the same time the rain did, but it didn't rain hard until we were too far down the river to turn back. It just got worse as we went along. It was cold and miserable and there weren't any ducks except one flock of mallards that flew off before we got in range just because I accidentally dropped a paddle. Six hours later we sat dripping wet in my pickup, shivering and savoring the hunt...sort of.

"Mac," I said, "I want you to know I don't have to kill a limit to enjoy a hunting trip. It's always good to get together with an old friend and ply the woods and waters in search of the elusive quarry."

Mac was trying to mix instant coffee into lukewarm water from his thermos, but the rain-water pouring from the brim of his hat was causing his cup to run over and he was so cold he couldn't hold it still.

"Take me to my car, he said without looking up, "so I can go home and forget I ever knew you!" He was just kidding of course. Why just the next year we killed a limit of wood ducks on the Piney. Mac really liked woodies back then, because those were the days of the point system and it only took two of the 90 point woodies to make a limit. A duck hunt always seems better when you can tell the guys back at the office you got a limit!

The point system, which has long since been abandoned, was just the thing for conscientious sportsmen who would refrain from shooting hens and those species not found in abundance. The point system really' helped me out one year in the early '80's when I was hunting in Iowa with a pair of cousins, John and Jake McNew. The night before, we were shooting a game of pool, and, since we didn't have enough money to make the game interesting, we decided on an unusual bet. The winner of the game would be allowed the first three shots of the following morning. The other two would wait patiently until those three empty hulls hit the water.

As so often happens when a good pool player is unfamiliar with the table, I wound up being one of the two losers. But Jake, the winning cousin, was dealt justice at shooting hours the next day when a single ten-point gadwall in the bush came barreling into the decoys and became a dead one hundred-point canvasback hen in the hand.

I doubt if Jake ever shoots first again. But then, those kind of things make lasting memories, perhaps more so than full game bags.

On another occasion in the eighties, I was hunting in the Nebraska sandhills with Nebraska's Chief of Wildlife, Ken Johnson, and Dave Meisner. We were hunting prairie chicken, but the day before we had experienced some good duck hunting on small ranch lakes. Returning to those lakes before dawn on the last day of our hunt, I was driving Dave's van when I saw a fluttering green-wing teal in the sandy road, which had obviously flown into an electrical line in the early morning fog. I stopped and retrieved the dying duck.

Ken commented that I was being a good conservationist by applying the teal to my daily limit. From his seat behind us, where he had been napping, I heard Dave snicker and say, "Conservationist! Heck, he's just thankful to find a dead one any time, the way he shoots."

When we left the lakes at mid-morning, and changed from chest-waders to leather boots in preparation for hunting prairie chicken in the hills, I took a photo of Dave and Ken with six or seven ducks of several species. But before I could shed my waders, Dave brought forth his camera and the little green-wing that I had found in the road.

"Here," he said, holding forth the biscuit-sized bird, "let me get a shot of you with your duck."

Yes, I have memories of many misty mornings on the marsh, but that last memory is strong. Dave Meisner, one of the finest men I ever knew, died suddenly a month or so before I began this book. Now, as I get older I realize how important old friends are, especially old duck hunting buddies... .and new ones. They say that in the course of a lifetime, a man is lucky if he can count just two or three close friends he can trust and depend on. If you're a duck hunter though, you've almost certainly got many more friends than that.. .and a world of treasured memories.

Dave Meisner in the sandhills of Nebraska, with Ram on his right and Mac to his left.

Chapter 13

A Family of Mallards

In northern Ontario, a drake and hen mallard drop from the skies on cupped wings. They pass over a high rocky ridge packed tight with sharp-tipped pines and glide against the wind toward the grassy bay across the lake.

In this region of Ontario, there are hundreds of lakes like this one. Lake Kiekewabic is still cold and lonely in early April. Some fishermen will fly into this isolated angler's paradise in weeks to come, but for now, Kiekewabic belongs to the wildlife that have survived the winter and the waterfowl that arrive daily on tired wings.

The mallard hen is at work on a nest within hours of her arrival, using her own down and grasses to form a 15-inch nest. The drake isn't much help, but he is ready to do his part later. The two have been together since November; they were among a large flock of mallards that spent much of the winter in South Dakota, then Kansas and Missouri.

This is the drake's first spring season as an adult, but the hen is old; this is her third nesting season. In October, she had paired with another drake which had fallen to the guns of hunters over a South Dakota pothole. In early November, the young drake had become her traveling partner.

In Missouri during a December snow storm, she had saved his white-ringed neck. Together, with a small group of mallards, they had winged low across a marsh when a hail call of resting mallards caused the whole flock to turn and seek them out. As they neared the large group of ducks loafing in the lee of a fringe of willows, the older, experienced hen instinctively knew they were not her own kind. She spotted the face in the blind and the gun barrel beside it.

As she veered away and gained altitude, the young drake followed, and most of the others followed him. There was the roar of shotguns, and stinging pellets broke the skin above one leg and along her back above the tail. She would survive that, but one of the flock was not so fortunate. They left him behind with a broken wing, flapping along the water's surface with a black dog in pursuit and gaining.

Now, on Lake Kiekewabic, the guns of the past winter were gone, and they prepared for the coming period of replenishing the species. Each morning, the pair would go through the courtship rituals and mating act, and each day the hen would lay one egg. Finally there were 12 of them, about normal for a hen mallard, who might lay as many as 13 eggs or as few as six or seven depending on her condition.

The incubation period will last just a day or two short of four weeks. The young drake will lose interest, finally, as the hen spends so much of her time on the nest. Occasionally, the drake will stay with the hen through the summer, but usually he does not. In this case, the drake leaves the lake entirely, and he'll never see this hen again. He will be miles away, molting, drab and colorless as well as flightless for nearly two months of the summer. During that time, he goes into seclusion, attempting to survive that period of vulnerability by hiding from predators.

The hen's nest is well hidden in high grasses at the end of a decaying log. The greatest predators of the nesting mallard on this lake are surely the ravens and raccoons. If either find the Kiekewabic nest, the hen can do little to defend it. If a nest is destroyed, the hen will usually leave, seek out her old mate or a new one, and renest. Of course, the mallard's greatest enemy during nesting periods is man. Agricultural operations and draining and burning destroy thousands of nests each year in the northern U.S. and Canada.

But Kiekewabic is a wilderness lake, and ravens are the first great threat here. The ducklings hatch, finally, in a two or three-hour period, even though more than two weeks separate the laying of the first and last egg. The embryos begin developing at the same time as incubation begins.

The Kiekewabic clutch numbers twelve young ducklings. Just over an hour after the last duckling hatches, they have dried completely, and "imprinting" has begun. Imprinting takes place during this first hour or so of life. At this time, the ducklings recognize the hen as their protector simply because of her movement. If you replace her with a goose, a chicken, or even a dog, the ducklings will accept that object as their mother. Substitute a moving roller skate, and after imprinting takes place, the ducklings will follow that skate wherever it can be pulled. Only after imprinting will the ducklings leave the nest, but then they will follow the hen anywhere.

There are times when mallard nests are quite some distance from the water, and there's probably no more dangerous time for the ducklings than that time spent moving to the water over dry land. Occasionally, one will be too weak to keep up, and he will eventually be left behind. Others may become lost in a tangle of vegetation or fall into a hole. If a predator spots the procession, there will often be losses, but on Lake Kiekewabic the distance to the water is not great and the the trip is uneventful.

Instinctively, the hen knows to seek out the shallowest water, with vegetation which provides camouflage and cover. The submerged weeds end 30 yards from the bank, and the water is deeper there. Lurking at the edge of those weeds are dozens of northern pike from three or four pounds to nearly fifteen pounds in weight. Any of them will gladly accept a duckling or two for dinner should the opportunity arise. The hen doesn't know what waits in the deeper water, but her instincts tell her to stay in the shallows.

At first, the young ducklings ravenously seek out

insects and aquatic larvae to sustain them, and mosquito larvae will make up much of the diet. Vegetation and seeds will slowly be added to that menu, and eventually become the main staple.

Growing rapidly, the young mallards are a month old when they see their first man. A fisherman from hundreds of miles south reaches for his camera as he sees them and snaps several pictures while his partner in the boat moves him slowly closer. Finally the old hen has had enough. She makes low, nervous, hoarse quacks, barely loud enough to perceive....instructions for her brood, which scatters into the heavy growth along the bank. The hen tries valiantly to fool the intruders; with a long labored

take-off along the water's surface, she heads toward the open lake. She splashes along, holding down one wing which is apparently broken. The fishermen have seen this act before, but they mean the family no harm. Smiling at her performance, they move on, and when they are some distance away, the hen returns to reassemble her brood.

It is something of a miracle that all twelve ducklings survive well into July. Nearly two months after hatching, the young are maturing rapidly, wing feathers developing enough for short flights. At nine weeks of age, they are flying easily.

In September, the hen finally feels the urge to move on. As the sun sets late in the day on Lake Kiekewabic, she takes to flight, heading westward. Behind her, the eight young drakes of the brood are beginning to show their colors. It is not a long flight, only 40 miles or so by air. If the young could feel emotion, it might be a sad flight — it is their last day with the old hen. They arrive at their destination in less than an hour, a large marsh near the border of Ontario and Manitoba, where hundreds and hundreds of waterfowl are coming together. This "staging area" is a melting pot. The young mallards suddenly lose the imprinting impulse that has caused them to follow their mother. They scatter and will take up with other adults. It is likely that some of this brood will winter in Illinois, southern Missouri, or Arkansas while others will pass through the Dakotas, Nebraska, and Kansas.

For a month or so, there's a great mass of ducks gathering on the marsh. They loaf and feed and group together in sudden practice flights, in which they circle the marsh and return again and again.

In late September, a sudden cold front passes through and, separated completely, the twelve Kiekewabic mallard ducklings rise with their individual flocks to begin a long night flight southward. The days have shortened, the colors of the earth have changed slowly. The wind is from the north, and flight is easy as migration begins. Among the older mallards, there's an urgency to travel, an appetite that can only be fulfilled by long hours of flight. Among the younger ducks there's an urge to follow those leaders wherever...

A little better than 20 years ago, ancestors of today's fall flights passed through the Ozark hills where I was beginning to gain my flight feathers as a hunter. I remember well the first wild mallard I ever shot at. He was only about two feet from my gun barrel, swimming about a foot and a half beneath the surface, a crippled drake that passed by the old wooden john-boat and a twelve-year-old who didn't know that a sixteen gauge charge of number fours wouldn't reach him. Dad may have seen some humor in that, but he didn't act like it. We had a talk about it on a nearby river gravel bar.

Maybe a year or so later, floating down that same river with my dad, I watched two groups of 50 or 60 mallards fall into a quiet eddy beneath a big white bluff, like leaves from a whirlwind. I think I knew back then that I wanted to be a waterfowl biologist, not knowing of course that waterfowl biologists are people who make grades two notches above the marks I brought home on my report card.

I got into college with that dream, and even graduated. But I lost my chance to be a waterfowl biologist when I got fed up with killing chickens and dissecting cats in Physiological Zoology. Soon afterward I learned that outdoor writers can work with waterfowl too, and you could fail darn near everything and still be one! I studied waterfowl with the same intensity. Every weekend I went back home and hunted ducks with dad!

About that time I heard of the work of Frank Bellrose, a scientist in Illinois who was studying mallard migration. Bellrose took large numbers of wild mallards from the

marshes of the Illinois river, strapped tiny flashlights to their legs, and turned them loose at night. He traced their flight by watching the flow of the flashlights, and found that on a clear night all the mallards flew straight back to their destination, each in nearly the same path. But on a cloudy night, mallards seemed disoriented and flew several directions. Bellrose developed a pretty solid argument that wild mallards use the stars to navigate their migration flights.

But I doubt if he ever gave any thought to what it must have been like for some hunter in southern Illinois later that fall who brought down a fat greenhead mallard only to find a flashlight attached to its leg. Scientists never think of such things; outdoor writers do. I can picture the poor fellow trying to convince his friends that old Blackie brought back a mallard with a flashlight held tightly in one webbed foot.

To a writer, it does not so much matter how the mallard migrates; it is just important that he does. After all, what good is the first November snow if there are no mallards before the storm? What beauty is there in a marsh sunset when there are no mallard flights silhouetted against the sky? Who cares if interest rates drop in December if there are no greenheads dropping into the blocks as a shivering Labrador looks on in silent anticipation?

Nine months after the hen mallard and her mate fell wearily to the grassy bay on Kiekewabic lake, a hunter stomps his feet inside his waders and blows a warm breath into cupped, numbed fingers. The big Labrador brings in the fat young drake that has fallen to his last shot, and he holds it high as his hunting partner snaps a picture.

"Hey, Al," he says, grinning, "reckon this is one of those little ducklings we took the pitchers of up in Ontario last June?"

The other hunter laughs, shakes his head, and says "Who knows?" Neither will say so, but they both kind of hope it isn't.

Chapter 14

Puddle Ducks

On a cold windy day in December, mallards arrived, riding a north gale that carried a winter storm across the plains. These were the last of them, late season mallards which had lingered in northern grain fields to the very last. Before them had come teal and wood ducks, pintails, baldpate and gadwall. Duck hunters had grown weary of the decoy-shy early-season mallards, and many had quit hunting. But on that day when tired mallards filled the high gray skies, and bobbing blocks invited them to stop and rest, the greenheads seemed to lose their wariness.

Every duck hunter lives for that sight. Flock after flock broke formation and spiraled down on cupped wings, side-slipping and plummeting rapidly from great heights, with no circling, no hesitation and no caution. We sat there and watched them descend, listening to the rush of wings through the air above us, watching as they dropped in with bright red legs extended. When you've seen that, you'll never again wonder why anyone would hunt ducks.

It is the mallard that makes up the bulk of the duck hunting in our region. They are the most numerous of the 'puddle-ducks', or surface feeding ducks, a group characterized by a straight-up ascent from the water, and legs that are fairly well forward on the body, well-adapted for walking. Divers, which will be discussed later in this book, seldom walk along the shores, with feet far back on their body in order to propel them well below the surface. They take to flight by running along the surface of the water.

Surface feeders, or puddle ducks, favor aquatic plants and acorns found near or in the water, but they also feed in grain fields. They eat so many things that they will surprise you at times with their diet. Once in the late 1970's when I lived in north Arkansas, heavy fall rains brought Bull Shoals lake way up, and all the tributaries were flooded, with water well up into the vegetation. Mallards were thick as flies in some of those flooded creeks, and I paddled my john-boat back up into one arm, jump-shooting ducks. One of the drake mallards I killed came up out of a pocket filled with debris, and he had earthworms in his beak and in his gullet. I guess it was quite a change from the grain they had feasted on up north, and what the heck, variety is the spice of life.

You'd be surprised too, at the size of the acorns we have found in a mallard or wood-duck crop (pronounced 'craw'). But they don't eat everything. I recently read an article by an outdoor writer who was convinced mallards were eating cockleburs. "They have a tremendously strong beak to mash up those cockleburs," he wrote. Several old veteran duck hunters got a laugh out of that. A duck beak has almost no strength whatsoever, and is not used to mash or masticate food. And yes, they can swallow an acorn, but not a cocklebur! Those spines would never get past the throat.

The food eaten by wild ducks passes into the crop, and into the the gizzard, where that muscular organ, filled with sand and grit, grinds up the seed and animal matter in the beginnings of the digestive process. The beak is effectively used not to mash or crush, but to sift and strain through the water.

The puddle ducks are excellent flyers, and the species which commonly migrate through the Ozarks are some of the most beautiful of all birds. Most mallards nest in the northern prairies from Nebraska up into Saskatchewan, but some nest in Midwest states well to the south. Most other puddle ducks do not. Their numbers rise and fall according to water conditions on northern breeding grounds, and they have dropped drastically from the '30's through the '80's because of agriculture draining of marshes and wetlands to make room for more crops and pasture. The conservation of wetlands, and several years of excessive rainfall in the northern prairies has reversed the situation, and the rebound of wild ducks has been remarkable at the turn of the century.

Of the puddle ducks, the mallard is the largest, weighing about two to three pounds with a wingspan of 36 inches. The pintail too is a large duck, but sleek and slender, weighing several ounces less than the mallard, though appearing to be nearly as large. Pintails, often called sprigs, don't quack as mallards do, they give forth a quiet whistle. They are fast flyers, and are particularly decoy wary, much less likely to fall into blocks than are mallards and teal. They circle and circle and circle, and sometimes just fly away.

Pintails nest well into the Arctic, much farther north than mallards and other puddle duck species, and the nesting grounds cover a larger area. Still, pintails have been particularly hard hit by the drought, and have showed a greater ten year decline than mallards and a slower rebound over the past few years. Pintails have been clocked at flight speeds of 90 m.p.h. with a tail wind, and up to 65 m.p.h. with no wind. These ducks actually do complete rolls in flight on occasion.

The gadwall is also a good-sized puddle duck, almost identical in size to a pintail, though shorter in length. They average about two pounds and have a 34 inch wingspan. Gadwalls, pintails, widgeons and teal often travel together in mixed flocks, and the larger species occasionally mix with mallards. Wild ducks occasionally cross, with offspring of spectacular beauty at times. You see pintail-mallard crosses more often than others, but occasionally there will be others, like the gadwall and mallard. Gadwalls quack like a mallard, and nest to the southern regions of Canada's prairie provinces. They are early migrators, fly at speeds of 45 to 50 m.ph. and are not particularly wary of decoys. In fact, they decoy so well that sometimes it's not much fun to take them. A gadwall is something of a pushover.

Widgeons, or baldpates, are sometimes confused with gadwall, especially hens and immature ducks. But mature drake widgeons are as beautiful as pintail drakes in their own way. Widgeons love wild celery and often hang around divers like canvasbacks, stealing the roots which divers bring up from the bottom. Like the pintails, the males have a soft whistle, but the hens also give forth a hoarse quack on occasion. They are smaller than gadwalls, and larger than teal, about the same body weight and size as the wood

duck. Like pintails, widgeons are fast, flying 50 to 60 m.p.h. They start to migrate early, but they move south slowly, and seem to take longer to migrate than other species.

Blue-winged and green-winged teal are the smallest ducks. The early-migrating blue-wings head south in late August and early September. Green-wings, are late migrators which come to decoys with little wariness when winter's worst blasts are upon us. They seldom make a pass at all, falling into the blocks without caution. They weigh only about twelve ounces, and the wing span is less than two feet, with a body only 13 or 14 inches long. Like the pintail, they nest well to the north, but their nesting range dips as far south as the Dakotas. When cleaned, the meat derived from a green-wing doesn't amount to much in quantity, so some hunters pass them up, but they are better eating than most puddle ducks, rivaled only by mallards.

Once many years back, my friend Rich Abdoler and I were hunting at the end of the season when the backwaters were beginning to ice up. Our decoys were really stuck in the ice, and we new it was just about time to break them out, sack them up and bid good-bye to the season. But late in the day, a little green-winged teal drake came streaking in, and hit the ice just short of our decoys. He thought he was settling into the water, but instead he hit hard and slid head over tail-feathers through most of the decoys, crashing into the last one, a big magnum drake mallard. He sat there awhile and then gathered himself to hop up on the decoy's head, where he surveyed the scene for a good five or ten minutes before flying away. He was a goofy-looking little fellow, sitting atop that decoy. I would have given anything if I had brought the camera that evening!

The poorest eating puddle duck is the shoveler, sometimes called a spoonbill. These are occasionally taken by midwestern hunters, but they aren't really common. Just a little larger than teal, they weigh 16 to 19 ounces, with a 32 inch wing span. Drakes are beautiful in the spring, of spectacular color, but it's well into the winter before the plumage becomes bright.

Like the teal, shovelers are fast and acrobatic in flight and they migrate early so the brightly colored males are seldom taken except in the deep south. The bill is long, and flattened, and widened at the tip. For it's size this duck has a larger bill than any other species and that gives it away in flight.

Wood ducks are "different" puddle ducks. They have the reputation, well deserved, of being the most beautiful waterfowl species. They nest in hollow trees. In fact they are the only ducks which nest in appreciable numbers in the Ozarks. Their nesting range extends from northern Louisiana all the way to southern Canada. But woodies winter deep in the south, and leave with the coming of the first real cold snap. They are, as the name implies, a duck which likes wooded, brushy water and small streams where acorns are plentiful.

Woodies weigh about 1 and 1/2 pounds and have a short body and short wingspan, 18 and 24 inches respectively. It is amazing to watch them weave and wind through tree tops in full flight, but they have more dexterity than speed. Woodies do more walking than other species, and are perching ducks, spending much of their time up on logs and snags over the water. They are excellent eating, but must be hunted much differently than other puddle ducks because they are not a duck of marshes and larger waters.

The one puddle duck you won't see much in the midwest anymore is the black duck, or black mallard as some call them. There were never many black ducks coming through the central flyway, but the Mississippi flyway; Illinois, East Arkansas and states to the east and south; occasionally saw fair numbers of them. Black ducks were, and still are, an eastern flyway species, and they nested in the more forested East Canada waters. Some ornithologists theorized that black ducks were a subspecies of mallard, and not a seperate species at all. They have always hybridized somewhat with the mallard, with fertile offspring. Usually, hybrid waterfowl are not fertile.

Black ducks look much like hen mallards, both the drake and the hen of the species. Drakes are little different in the coloration of the beak, but lots of hunters bag an occasional black duck and think it's just a dark mallard hen. Black ducks are very dark, but instead of the blue wing patch found on the mallard, their wing patch is a deep purple color. The belly is very dark, and looks almost black when they pass over in contrast to the light underside of the mallard. The underneath sides of the wings have a silvery-gray appearance, and the beaks have a greenish yellow cast, rather than the bright yellow of the mallard.

There is no puddle duck species so wary and cautious as the black duck. They will seldom, almost never, come to decoys in a hurry as mallards will sometimes do. They will circle and circle and circle, and then maybe never commit themselves. And if you see a good-sized flock, you'll know they are black ducks not only from that shyness....you'll think you're looking at a flock of very dark hen mallards and wonder why there isn't a drake in the bunch.

Perhaps black ducks are declining even yet, when other ducks are increasing, because mallards are now moving into the East Canada waterways where the black duck nests, and hybridizing the species out of existence.

133

Chapter 15

Wood Ducks

Wh, hile driving on a gravel ridge-top road one recent spring day we were delayed by a procession of wild ducks, a mother and nine little balls of fluff. We were a mile from the river. Those little wood ducks had a long trip ahead of them, but the hen knew where she was going. By midday, they would be cooling their heels in the current of an Ozark stream where they would grow up...in only a matter of weeks.

The first ducks I hunted were woodies. I was only twelve years old at the time, and I remember those early days with fondness. But the truth is, I've never seen wood duck populations higher than they are today as we enter a new century.

Fifty or sixty years ago, wildlife people thought that wood ducks might become extinct. Their decline began in the early 1900s, in part because of heavy commercial hunting. But modern biologists believe that the destruction of bottomland hardwoods during the World War I era had much to do with the wood duck's decline. Hollow trees are important to many birds and mammals, and when the only goal of timber managers is board feet of lumber, species like the wood duck suffer. Without nesting sites, they hit rock-bottom populations by 1920.

In 1918, wood ducks became a protected species in both the United States and Canada, one of the first results of the migratory bird treaty. It would not be legal to harvest woodies again until 1941. The 23 years of protection worked, but nature required a helping hand.

One man in particular had a great deal to do with the comeback of wood ducks. Dr. Donald Carter of the New York

Museum of Natural History obtained a federal permit to acquire and incubate wood duck eggs. From his home near a wetland area of New Jersey, Carter released hundreds of wood ducks every year. But adult woodies still needed habitat to multiply.

Trees do not grow old and hollow for nesting purposes within a few decades. So naturalists and biologists across the Midwest encouraged the construction of wood duck boxes to aid successful nesting. Most of this encouragement was in the form of example. They built the boxes and hung them in trees. Soon, however, many waterfowl hunters were following the act.

Eventually, tens of thousands of boxes were hung. You can find them throughout the midwest today in isolated spots on little-used waterways. Some of these boxes have remained for decades, supporting nests over and over again.

Like other ducks, woodies migrate. But they are unique in that they may nest anywhere from southern Canada to Louisiana. Thousands of them raise their young in the Ozark region, considering it to-be the equivalent of the far north. Until the first cold spell of November drives them out, wood ducks—those hatched here and those migrating from the north—are abundant.

The mother wood duck that we encountered high on the ridge was not an extreme oddity. Hens often nest a mile or two from the water. I once saw a hen wood duck and her brood walk along a busy thoroughfare in North Little Rock as they headed toward the Arkansas River more than a mile away.

Wood ducks begin nesting in April. Drakes and hens both play a part in finding a nesting site. Along midwestern waterways, hollow sycamores proved perfect cavities. Farther north, other waterfowl such as hooded mergansers and buffleheads compete with wood ducks for nesting cavities. Hooded merganser hens, however, have been known to share a nest with wood duck hens, incubating and hatching the young of both. But the wood duck's biggest competition comes from squirrels and woodpeckers. A couple of years ago, a turkey hunter sat beneath a large sycamore during April. The hunter watched a wood duck hen fly to an opening in the trunk and stick her head in to investigate. After a flurry of activity, the wood duck fell dead, bitten through the skull by a fox squirrel.

A wood duck needs an opening of nearly four inches and about 50 square inches of floor space within the cavity. The hen will lay her eggs early in the morning over a two-week period, using no nest material except down from her breast and belly. She'll lay nine to twelve eggs on the average, and the drake leaves her when incubation begins. During the nesting period, raccoons are the wood duck's biggest enemy, they love the eggs.

After hatching, ducklings spend only a few hours inside the nest cavity. Early in the morning of the first day, the hen leaves the cavity to coax the young out. She sits on a nearby limb or flies to the ground and calls softly. John Audubon once claimed that the hens carried their ducklings from the nest to the ground, but I don't know anyone who has seen that happen, and I don't believe it does.

I've seen them leave the nest on several occasions, and each time the tiny ducklings came down as if they had lost their balance and had fallen head over heels. Sometimes it's a long way to the ground, but the chicks are so small and fluffy they aren't injured.

When you see a mother woodie and her young along a small stream or river, you might think that the small ducklings' chances of survival are slim. But when you see them scatter and melt into their surroundings, you realize why wood ducks have thrived and increased in recent years. If only all game birds could hatch so many young and protect them as well...

Ducklings eat everything they can catch and swallow. Aquatic and terrestrial insects make up the bulk of their diet. Mature wood ducks, however, consume 90 percent plant matter—one reason why they are near the top of the list for the dinner table.

Wood ducks are more like geese than ducks when it comes to using their legs. They walk easily and will leave the water to walk into nearby cornfields to feed. Only one other food is as tasty as corn to woodies... acorns. Small creeks often hold large numbers of wood ducks during the fall when acorns are plentiful along the bottom lands.

They are adept at flying through mazes of branches, and they are the only species I have observed that alight as a flock on logs and limbs.

I don't know if that the federal people who assign bag limits for waterfowl have a handle on the number of wood ducks in the Midwest today. Because they nest over the entire Mississippi flyway and way up into Canada, and not just in particular areas, calculating wood duck numbers is next to impossible. With wood duck numbers so high, a daily bag limit of three drakes would not hurt the population.

Wood ducks are numerous in the the Midwest from mid-October to mid-November, which means you only get to hunt them for the first couple of weeks of the duck season. When some serious cold weather moves in, woodducks waste no time leaving. But early in the season, wood ducks provide easy, enjoyable hunting.

On larger rivers, woodies will be flying early and late, especially on weekends when boaters are stirring them up. They don't decoy like mallards, but they do come in, usually only for one pass.

They are also found near rivers of almost any size, or on ponds and marshes where vegetation or trees are near the water. And they can maneuver so well through the branches that they provide some of the most challenging wingshooting I've experienced.

I'll never forget the sight of hundreds of woodies twisting through the trees, five or six at a time. That's the way it was in Iowa years back when that state opened an early duck season and it was almost all wood duck hunting.

I had a big yellow Labrador back then named Brown-Eyed Beau, and he was so young and inexperienced you never knew what to expect of him. We went to Iowa in late September to hunt with my cousins, the McNew brothers, who knew where the woodies were thick. It was a flooded bottomland north of Des Moines about 40 miles, a place where it was easy to hide and where Beau could watch the wood ducks coming in to feed on acorns. When someone got lucky and dropped one, Beau could see it all, and he was really learning fast. The high point of the morning came when Jake McNew hit a drake wood duck and watched it sail out of the bottoms across a harvested cornfield, where it finally went down. We took Beau out to try to find it, but none of us figured he would. The big yellow pup showed us what a nose he had by searching out the woodie completely hidden in a clump of vegetation at least 20 yards from where we thought he had fallen.

We had great wood duck hunting in Iowa, in those wooded, shallow sloughs surrounded by cornfields. They were areas virtually unhunted, and they weren't just attractions for migrating ducks, they were hatcheries. Tremendous numbers of wood ducks are hatched there each year because woodies don't need or want big waters. They are at home on the smallest of creeks, the shallowest of brushy backwaters.

During the summer, they don't seem very wary. In fact, some have said they thought the wood duck decline was due, in part, to a lack of wariness that other waterfowl species have. I don't buy that. While growing up , I spent

too many years hunting wood ducks along the Big Piney River which were ready to fly at the slightest unnatural sound or sight. It was never easy to float within range of a flock of wood ducks, and sometimes they were nearly impossible to see if they were resting in a brushy spot, or sitting in amongst the limbs of a fallen tree. For every instance when we sneaked within gun range, there was another flock which flushed at 60 yards.

Only 19 years after they reopened the season on wood ducks, I was floating the Big Piney with my Dad when a pair of wood ducks swam out away from a submerged root wad and began to swim away. They were suspicious of that oak and maple blind attached to the front of our old wooden john-boat, and they wasted no time swimming through a shoal and out of sight around a gravel point downstream.

"They saw us," Dad whispered, as he back paddled to the nearest bank, "but I've got an idea."

Until that day, I had never killed a flying duck. I had busted my share of them sitting on the water, and I had wasted lots of shells trying to hit one flying, but I wasn't a very good shot at the age of twelve. Having just turned 13, I had given up the old single shot hammer gun, and owned a used Model twelve Winchester with a short-barrel, and a cut down stock. With three shots from that old pump-gun, I just knew I would be a better duck hunter. Dad had his doubts, but he told me to wait there in the boat while he sneaked down the river and surprised those two woodies. If he didn't get a good shot, at least he would flush them back upstream toward me and I could waste another shell or two as they flew past.

So I waited there, wishing I could shoot like Dad. When he shouldered that old '97 Winchester pump gun those ducks were in trouble. Minutes later, I heard one shot downstream and I got ready, not really expecting any action. Suddenly, two ducks appeared before me, sweeping upstream just below treetop level. When they were nearly upon me, I tried to lead the first one several feet and swing on it at the same time, just like Dad had tried to teach me. At the right time, I squeezed off a shot, and one of the drakes folded and plunged headlong into the river before me. It may have even been the one I was shooting at!

By the end of the season, I had downed several flying

My first ducks were wood ducks on the Big Piney.

wood ducks and while Dad hoped for late season mallards, I lived for a flock of unseen wood ducks, flushing from a pocket or slough or a fallen tree along the river as we floated past. And I will never forget the day that Dad waited in the boat while I slipped back up into a little creek that fed the Piney. A small pocket there beneath towering oaks always held wood ducks, but not that day. As I stood there wondering why, I heard the shriek of an old hen, looked up, and saw three woodies coming through the treetops, wings set for that little creek pocket. In all my years I will never forget the beauty of those speeding ducks dodging branches at 150 miles per hour, gliding in on top of me. Little wonder I would become addicted to ducks over decoys in a few years.

They were 35 yards away when I emptied my pump gun, and 150 yards away when my last empty hull hit the water — or so it seemed. I hadn't pulled a feather. At fifteen years of age, I had grown somewhat proud of my shooting —to the point of bragging a little on occasion. As I waded back toward the river and the john-boat, I wondered what I was going to tell Dad.

I found out later that wood ducks don't really fly 150 miles an hour. But when they're coming through the treetops, it looks like it. On first impulse, you want to lead an incoming wood duck about 20 yards.

They might be an easier target over a pothole in a cornfield, but where there are branches and flooded timber overhead, they are dodging and dipping and darn near impossible to intercept.

They don't really care too much for your decoys, if you want to hunt woodies, you have to hunt them where they rest or feed and that's usually a chore. You should get ready to expend round after round trying to hit a duck that flies fast and crooked and hides behind limbs. In wood duck haunts I have hunted, the branches are filled with shot.

Chapter 16

Trash Ducks

In September a waterfowler can warm up on blue-winged teal. But when a true and devout duck hunter goes teal hunting, its like Arnold Palmer playing miniature golf...Hank Aaron playing wiffle ball...Mario Andretti driving a go-cart.

I do it though, because it has been months since I've lured ducks across my decoys. When the mid-morning heat becomes too much, my Labrador and I return to my basement retreat. There are no windows there and it is cool, a place where you can pretend there's a snowstorm going on outside.

My antique guns are kept there, all two of them, on the same wall with my game bird collection, more ducks than anything else.

In September the corners of my retreat are stacked with duck decoys that need repair, shotgun shells that need sorting and old waders that must be patched. But the best thing about my basement retreat is the pictures: paintings of bluebills riding a blizzard, mallards settling into the backwaters of Mississippi bottom land pin oaks, Canada geese against a winter sunset. There are green-winged teal in a prairie pothole, wood ducks preening on an Ozark slough.

I can lie on the couch, stare at those paintings for awhile and actually smell the burnt gunpowder, actually see them flying away after I've missed.

You never really see it like the artist paints it, but in the summer, all a duck-hunter can do is dream about the coming fall. I lie on my couch and stare at the bluebills in the snowstorm. In my mind I lead the oncoming drake just right, and he folds perfectly as I squeeze the trigger. Fat chance. Bluebills have to be painted because they are too fast to be photographed, and way too fast to be hunted.

In Canada a few years ago we hunted bluebills on Lake of the Woods with an Ojibway guide who watched small squadrons pour across our decoys a few feet ahead of our shot patterns. He said it would be better when the bad weather came. Flocks would have 200, 300 ducks, maybe more. "Then", he said seriously, "you could get some better!"

Scaup and ringnecks are collectively known as blackjacks in the south. I will never forget one "blackjack" hunt I had in Arkansas a few years back. It was on a public hunting area just off the Arkansas river not far from Oklahoma. It was early January, and you've got to remember I was young then, and not as good a wing shot as I have since become after fifteen years of shooting and a dump truck full of empty shot shell hulls.

Another thing; we were hunting from a small boat that bobbed around like a cork, with the wind blowing and the waves crashing.

At any rate there was a federal agent sitting across the marsh listening to us shoot. When we pulled our boat out just after dark, he was waiting, licking his chops like a hound under the dinner table. Before we were close to the parking lot he pounced on us and made us unload everything. He looked in each decoy bag, he looked under boat seats, he made us pull the straw out of the bottom of the boat and sift through it, then he checked our waders.

Finally he sat down on the levee and his shoulders sagged. He had the look of that cartoon coyote that chases a roadrunner every Saturday morning on T.V. "You don't even have a limit!" he exclaimed, shaking his head. "How in the devil could anybody shoot that much, that often and not even get a limit?"

John looked at me and I looked at him. Our faces lifted. It wasn't that we looked like market hunters, it was all that shooting we had done.

"Blackjacks," I told him. "We were shooting at black-jacks. There were two or three flocks and they just kept coming back around that last thirty minutes or so!"

The agent got to his feet and shuffled through our assortment of mallards, teal, and ringnecks. "You only got three blackjacks," he said. It sounded more like a statement than a question.

John looked off into the darkness. "Well, yeah," I said, "but I think I hit one pretty hard that just kept going."

The agent headed off into the marsh. As he sloshed along I could hear him mumbling something about "trash ducks."

That's what really made me mad. Here I had spent a box and a half of shells on those blackjacks and he's call-ing 'em trash ducks.

I don't know why, but to this day that term gets under my skin. There are no trash ducks, just ducks. Now coots and mergansers aren't really ducks, so when you lump most of the other divers in that category you're doing a dis-service to some very beautiful and deserving species of waterfowl. Ringneck, scaup, bufflehead, goldeneye, red-heads and even canvasbacks: these are the ones most often looked down upon by those who consider the mallard on a higher plane than all other ducks just because a scaup doesn't come to a high-ball. If there is a more beautiful duck anywhere than a drake bufflehead or goldeneye, I'll eat it (just bring it to me cleaned and picked).

And are we to relish the wild mallard on the table mere-ly because it is better eating to some degree? Who among us rates a barnyard chicken above the wild mallard just because of drumsticks and wishbones?

These "divers" are separated from "puddle ducks" mostly by the method they take to flight. For someone who doesn't recognize the difference, the easiest explanation is that when a puddle duck takes to flight, it pushes against the water with its wings and springs straight up. When a puddle duck is 30 feet above the water, he may be almost directly above the spot where he was sitting. A diving duck of course, has to get a run at it to get off the water. He uses his feet to propel him along the surface until the wings get him airborne. And while the puddle ducks can walk around quite well, and do so, the divers do not walk well and seldom attempt it. Their legs are situated well back on the body and are best used for swimming and diving.

Some duck hunters erroneously label divers as "fish eaters." But all ducks, even puddle ducks, eat some fish. The divers as a rule eat a higher percentage of "animal matter," but usually fish

do not make up the bulk of that. The goldeneye, for instance, dives beneath the surface to overturn stones, stir up the bottom and feed on insect larvae, crustaceans and mollusks. It certainly will eat small fish, but about 25 percent of the goldeneye's diet is plant foods such a pondweed, smartweed and wild celery.

Of the divers I have mentioned, the goldeneye and buf-

Hunter with a ringneck drake in winter plumage.

flehead eat the most animal matter. Both consume 70 to 80 percent animal matter, but the tiny bufflehead favors insects and aquatic larvae over fish. Of the divers, these two are probably the least desirable on the dinner table. Goldeneye and bufflehead taken on a waterfowl hunt should be cleaned and held in a special spot in the freezer for those occasions when the boss drops in for dinner.

The two species of scaups, lesser and greater, probably get a bum rap. The diet of the lesser scaup is 50 to 60 percent plant matter, and the greater scaup close to that. Sometimes these ducks are fat as butterballs, and very palatable, depending on where they are and what they've eaten.

The ringneck duck is confused with the scaup by the novice hunter, but in feeding habits, the ringneck is closer to the redhead. Ringnecks, redheads and canvasbacks eat 80 to 90 percent vegetable matter. They may be known as divers, but they dive for vegetation. These three are excellent eating. The canvasback has long been considered to be the best eating of all waterfowl in New England and along the east coast.

Some say the canvasback even got its name back in the early days of market hunting when the ducks were transported in canvas bags which the shipper wanted returned. On each bag these instructions were printed in bold lettering: "Send canvas back!". Anyway, putting canvasbacks in the category of "trash ducks" is like hitching the Kentucky Derby winner to a plow.

East Coast hunters of yesteryear looked down their noses at everything but canvasbacks. They used large rafts of decoys, and canvasbacks responded well to the large spreads.

They are a diver, a wildfowl particularly fond of large open bays, and as the years have passed, they have grown particularly wary. Yet many years ago, canvasbacks and redheads were often lured into gun range by "Tolling Dogs" along the east coast.

Tolling dogs are small red dogs taught to chase and play with a stick along the shoreline. Diving ducks well out into the bays were curious enough to swim in close to the tollers. I understand this technique is still being used to some extent in Canada, and red Tolling Dogs are recognized as a distinct breed and still being raised today. Just a year or so ago I ran into some people from St. Louis who were hunting ducks in western Missouri and had a pair of the dogs they were hunting with. They of course were just using them as retrievers.

Overshooting contributed greatly to the decline of canvasbacks and redheads, but it was the great loss of nesting habitat that has kept them from regrouping. And while they have been rebounding in recent years, they are doing so at a much smaller rate of increase than the puddle ducks.

It's not too difficult to recognize the canvasback, but at times redheads can fool anyone. Several years ago, four of us hunted ducks on western Missouri's Truman Lake, back in a flat flooded field that was anything but diver habitat. We were hunting from my 18-foot duck boat on that occasion because the area was flooded and the water was deep where we were hunting. The boat was covered by my portable blind and plenty big enough for four hunters. The hunting was good that morning, but the weather wasn't. The rain fell lightly at first but by 10 a.m. was coming down hard with the temperature at about 35 degrees. Despite rain gear, we began to get wet and felt miserable.

Everyone had three mallard drakes, and we had lost some cripples in spite of the two retrievers in the boat. It was one of those days. We were all thinking about going in to a warm fire when a good-sized flock of divers swept around us and headed into the decoys on the first pass.

I thought of nothing but ringnecks and in the rain I didn't see a redhead until the first volley had been fired. With four ducks on the water, we had a limit, but we four experienced duck hunters were a little embarrassed that day to finish out with the redheads. In that time, they were hard pressed and you were only allowed one. Back in that flooded pocket we had never expected to see divers. I'll always have a good story to tell about that redhead drake that went in my game bird collection. And no one had better ever refer to him as a trash duck.

Redheads and goldeneyes fly up to fifty miles per hour but canvasbacks, according to the people who are supposed to know, are the fastest of all ducks flying from 70 to 75 m.p.h. without a wind. When they are migrating with some wind behind them they do travel faster than that, maybe at times covering 100 miles an hour after all. But those early naturalists who claimed that canvasbacks were sweeping over decoys at 100 miles per hour had to be hunting them....lots of ducks fly faster when you are missing them.

As stated earlier, all diving ducks have their legs in the wrong place when it comes to walking so you don't see them hiking along the shore very often. They use their legs for diving. Canvasbacks are known to dive 20 feet or more for wild celery root, while puddle duck species wait on the surface and try to steal a meal from them. Widgeons, or baldpates, are notorious for that. There have been accounts of goldeneyes diving to depths of 40 feet, and it is a fact that a crippled diver is a tough duck to find because of his ability to dive and swim so far beneath the water.

Goldeneyes use their wings as well as their feet to swim beneath water, and they can really put some distance behind them. A crippled diver on the water should be dispatched with a second shot as quickly as possible.

The wariness exhibited by canvasbacks is not shared by redheads and ringnecks. Scaup, goldeneyes and buffleheads will decoy fairly well if you have large spreads of diver decoys with black and white markings. Divers are attracted to large spreads. They are not as quick to come to a small number of decoys. Mallard decoys in large numbers will pull them in, but it's good to have some bluebill decoys bunched up where they are easy to see.

The key to hunting diving ducks is not only large blocks of decoys, but also knowing the best locations to use them. Divers are open water ducks, and while they'll occasionally show up anywhere, as those redheads did in Missouri that year, they prefer big open water. A little wind is no problem.

As a rule, it's not at all difficult to distinguish the different species. Buffleheads and green-winged teal are the smallest of the waterfowl, weighing from twelve ounces to one pound, with a wing span just under two feet. The bufflehead's distinguishing mark is the large white crest beginning below the eye, and the bufflehead's feet are pink.

The canvasback, of course, is one of the largest wild ducks in North America; a little heavier than the mallard, but a bit shorter with less of a wing span that of the greenhead. The canvasback drake has a brownish-red head and a black beak that slopes high from the forehead. The gray weave in the white back looks like canvas I guess, just a little. Maybe that's where the name really came from. The breast and tail are black, and the eye is red.

The redhead drake has a similar look, but the eyes are yellowish-orange, the beak gray with a black tip, and the forehead rounds down to the beak. The coloration of the head is also a reddish brown, but in bright sunlight, you'll catch the light off of it just right and call it red.

The scaups — greater and lesser — are very similar. The greater scaup is a little bigger, a little more spectacularly marked as far as the white back and sides are concerned. The lesser scaup has more gray in the feathers on the back. Both species have bright yellow eyes, and a blue beak that lumps them together under the common name "bluebill." The feet are also blue, or bluish gray. The greater scaup has a black head with a green sheen in the right light, while the head of the lesser scaup has a purplish sheen.

Remarkably, you can differentiate between the two species of goldeneyes the same way. The Barrow's golden-

eye has a purplish sheen to the head; the common goldeneye has a greenish sheen. Both species have a white spot
between the eye and beak. The spot is round on the common goldeneye, and more of a crescent on the Barrow's
goldeneye. Both birds have black beaks and yellow-gold
eyes with light orange feet. But the common goldeneye has
a great deal more white on the side than the Barrow's.

Certainly the most misidentified diver species is the
ringneck, so named because of a light brownish-red ring
around the neck. The drake can be spectacular with black
breast and back and snow white sides. The head is unusual, high at the back of the skull. The eyes are yellow, but
the beak is very distinctive. There's white trim at the base
and a half-inch-wide white band toward the tip. They are
nicknamed "blackjacks" and they are indeed black on top
unlike the scaups. But they too are lumped in that collective category of "bluebills."

It's the ringneck that circles decoys two or three times
after being fired upon. Those are the ducks that got my
friend and me in hot water with that federal agent in
Arkansas back in the early seventies.

But I don't look at the bluebills and the other divers as
a dumb ducks like some other hunters do. I figure they are
just a bit more daring than the others. A taxidermist from
Columbia, Missouri, told me about hunting divers on the
Texas coast. He said he was out in his layout boat, and had
thrown the decoy bags on the shore of a small island behind
him. A redhead drake flew in, landed and swam around his
boat to the bank where it climbed upon a decoy bag and
went to sleep. Later, the hunter emptied his gun at a flock
of scaup, and was surprised to see the redhead still sitting
on the decoy bag after all the hulls had hit the water.

He said at first he figured the redhead was demon-
strating how dumb the species actually is. But then he
decided maybe the duck wasn't so dumb. After all, who's
gonna shoot at his own decoy bag?

A flock of greater scaup.

Chapter 17

Born of Blizzards

Wissen bluebills come across a set of decoys, you wonder why there isn't a vapor trail behind them. They streak
past low and quick like a squadron of fighter jets on a straf-
ing run. Compared to bluebills, a flock of mallards settling
into your blocks are duck soup... like shooting balloons
on a summer breeze. Bluebills are borne of gales and
nor'westers and early blizzards.

I first experienced bluebill hunting in Arkansas 25
years ago, when some friends and I were hunting ducks
in early January along the Arkansas River near the Holla
Bend Refuge. Floodwaters had created some large deep potholes along some creeks with adjacent crop land and we
would pull a small boat through the shallows, then paddle to a row of submerged willows where we could become
fairly effectively hidden. Mallards and puddle ducks were
tough to fool that late in the season, but we were having
good luck one afternoon until the ringnecks showed up. A
flock of fifteen or so swept past us in easy range, but surprised us so much we didn't get off a shot.

My hunting partner called them blackjacks, and knew
them better than I. "Get ready," he said, "that was just their
first pass."

Sure enough, they swung wide and bore down upon
us a second time, straight into the teeth of full-choke twelve
gauges and high-brass loads. The little valley echoed with
the blasts, and one duck plummeted to the surface. The
flock climbed and swept in a long wide arc, then wheeled
around and came back, hell-bent for that little pothole filled
with fake ducks.

The end result was three passes, twelve empty shotshell hulls and three ringnecks. Plus a great deal of confusion has to who dropped what. I said that day I'd just as soon not see any more ringnecks Still and all, every time we drew a flock across our blocks we squeezed the shotguns a little tighter and intensified our concentration, knowing we were about to be tested a few notches above normal. It was like a hitter knowing he was about to bat against Nolan Ryan. You hunted mallards for relaxation and enjoyment.... you hunted ringnecks for challenge and excitement.. and revenge

Ringnecks are not the real bluebills that the northern hunters refer to. They are just one of two species which fit into the collective term of "bluebills". Greater and lesser scaup are the "real" bluebills. Ringnecks migrate before the scaup, and are very similar in the way they come across the decoys.

Who would have thought back then, that someday we'd set forth to hunt bluebills only. It happened about 20 years ago when Mike Dodson and I made our first trip to Lake of the Woods in Canada, spending most of the week at a resort north of Baudette, Minnesota. It was a mid-October trip arranged by some other friends who had been there before and we were to hunt grouse and ducks and fish a little.

Mike and I were pretty high on the duck hunting angle, so the first day they sent us out with an old Ojibway guide in a small V-bottom boat to cross white-caps that absolutely scared us to death. But the guide knew what he was doing, and an hour after

first light he set out blue-bill decoys off a point way back in tributary where wild rice was growing. It was a beautiful remote widerness spot sheltered from the wind, but Mike and I were skeptical. Where we had been hunting ducks, you always saw ducks, flying around, sitting here and there.... That day, we hadn't seen a duck anywhere.

Our guide didn't say much, but he seemed to have confidence. We built a blind on a flat rock several feet above the water, overlooking our decoys on the end of that point.

And then we sat there for an hour with no action.

The old Ojibway said to be patient. And sure enough, about ten o'clock that morning, a flight of about 20 ring-necks caught us by surprise. Not that we didn't get off a shot or two, we did. But we hadn't been ready for the fast-ball, especially a Nolan Ryan fast ball, and we struck out.

From that point on, the action was pretty regular. We learned not to look high in the sky for those ring-necked rockets. But if you looked way out into the bay, you could see them coming like a swarm of gnats, only 20 or 30 feet above the water, and they'd be over your blocks in a heart-beat. We learned to lead the individual ducks that day, rather than shoot at the entire flock. By early afternoon, when the flights of bluebills let up a little, we had a limit of 18 for the three of us. Rambunctious, my chocolate Labrador, had a great time that day. He would sit up there behind us on that flat spot and watch the ducks come in, the best view he had ever had of the action. And by the time it was over, he had retrieved more ducks than he had ever retrieved before in his young life. Only two years old at the time, Ram learned more about his work that week than he had learned during the entire season the year before.

Lake of the Woods is, and has been for many years, one of the best bluebill waters in North America. It is a great staging area for scaup and ringnecks, though the two sel-dom arrive there together. Usually the scaup are ten days to two weeks behind the ringnecks, sometimes more. The ringnecks come in and inhabit the backwaters of the bays, way up in the end of the tributaries where the wild rice is thick and beaver dams are numerous, the kind of places where the moose wade out and feed up to their bellies in the water. Usually there are quite a few mallards back in those spots with the ringnecks, and the season opens in mid-September. The local Canadians hit those spots until the mallards leave.

Returning from a goose hunt in Manitoba many years back, I drove down into the east side of the Lake of the

Woods to fish a day or so with some friends who own a lodge at Nestor Falls. The ringnecks were especially thick that year, so one evening I took old Ram and a small boat and motored back into a deep bay to a wild rice patch. It was absolutely unforgettable in it's beauty. I felt as if we had gone back in time a couple of hundred years and imagined that the first French explorers and trappers had seen the Lake of the Woods just like it was that afternoon. The first of my ancestors that I know about was such a Frenchman whose name in that time was spelled Dableaumonte'. My grandfather told me that another ancestor by the name of Mallory had married a Cree Indian woman from that area in Canada.

I got back into that cove early, just my Lab and I, and I enjoyed being there, even if there were no ducks. And I wondered what those early people were like, how they possibly could have survived the winters there. The Lake of the Woods is so vast, so complicated with it's hundreds of islands and bays, it is hard to imagine that the Indian guides who work there, and many of the Canadians can cross the lake, and find any place they wish to find day or night. This is a body of water perhaps 100 miles long and 40 miles wide with so many inlets and narrows and islands I have to take a map to go out three or four miles.

In October, the fishing is great, and the fall colors are beyond any description I am capable of. That afternoon years ago, as Ram and I sat waiting, I asolutely forgot everything in the peacefulness of that wilderness bay. And as I did, I forgot about the ringnecks we were there to hunt. About an hour after we got there, the first flock came in with a sudden roar of wings. Not the roar of a lion, but the roar you hear when complete stillness is interrupted by the wind over 30 sets of wings. They were gone before I could react, and they swung in, climbed high over the ridge, wheeled and dived back upon us. That time, I was ready. I lead the closest one, and he hurtled into the decoys when I squeezed the trigger. A second duck, just beyond him, also intercepted the shot pattern and I had two ducks on the water. In the next hour, they came in flocks of eight or ten, fifteen or twenty. At first I held Ram back, not wanting him to be out there while ringnecks were above him. But then I saw an otter retrieve one of my ducks, so I let my Lab get the rest of them.

We had a limit of ringnecks well before dark, but we stayed to watch and enjoy the show. October never arrives that I don't think of that bay, even when I can't get there. And I can still see it distinctly after all these years.

There are few people in the Lake of the Woods area who watch the arrival and departure of the bluebills like Alan Meline of Nestor Falls, Ontario. Meline has lived in the region all of his life and is a full-time hunting and fishing guide on Lake of the Woods. His father was a Provincial Game Ranger there, and Alan learned all about the area following his dad around as a boy. But his father wasn't able to take Alan duck-hunting much because of his job. A cousin who was a few years older was an avid duck hunter, and Alan learned about bluebill hunting from him. It followed, since he knew the lake so well from the trips with his dad, that Alan would be guiding waterfowlers at a young age. He remembers that he was fourteen years old the first time he took hunters out on the big lake to hunt bluebills, and he was paid fourteen dollars. Back then, boats were the old V-bottom type and motors were usually 25 horsepower or less. That was about 1950. Alan still guides duck hunters on Lake of the Woods, and he says it's better today than it was then.

We hunted with him a day or two a couple of years back, and we reached a remote bay in one of his big Lund fishing boats powered by a 150 horsepower motor. He just put a canoe inside it, and with hunters, guns, decoys and Reba, his Chesapeake Bay Retriever, we must have journeyed eight or nine miles out. We stopped at a beaver dam, put the canoe out on the other side of it, and paddled back into an otherwise unreachable pond where mallards and ringnecks were loafing.

Reba had her work cut out for her, but she did one heck of a job. There were six ducks on the water once, and she got all of them but one. A ringneck drifted out quite aways past the decoys while she worked, and an eagle, watching from a perch across the pond, swept down to grasp it in his talons and added it to his own limit. We yelled

Alan Meline and Reba.

at him, but he ignored us. Alan said it happens often when you hunt those bays. Eagles and otters have to eat too.

We were gone when October 20 rolled around. Meline keeps telling me we come and go too early. Somewhere in that third week of October, most of the ducks are gone too, and that's when the real duck hunting begins, according to Alan. The first real blizzards begin to take shape to the north, the wild rice bays and beaver ponds freeze over and only the big lake is open. Then they come, in only one or two days, thousands upon thousands of scaup, the real bluebills Canadian hunters are waiting for.

"Sometimes out in the open lake to the west of us, in the area of Big Traverse Bay, there will be rafts of ducks from 70 to 110 thousand," he said. "They come when the temperature dives and it's snowing and the wind is cold and the weather is brutal."

Meline hunts the islands out in the lake, and he says the best places are those islands out away from the others, with as much open water as possible. The worse the weather gets, the better the hunting is, as small groups leave the big flock and swarm the Lake of the Woods looking for food.

"You set out 40 or 50 decoys and the water is usually pretty deep off those island points so you set out eight or nine together on one long line, rather than 40 decoys with 30 feet of line on each."

It's cold and snowy and blustery when the 'bills are in, but Alan says the gun barrels get hot, and those scaup are moving on when they come over decoys. Ringneck hunting is for softies, Meline says. "Come back in late October," he keeps telling me, "when winter sets in and the duck hunting begins."

I guess, just once at least, I'm going to have to go, and see what real diver hunting is all about. But how could it beat what I've seen.... in early October when the woods are painted and the lake is so beautiful it is awesome in it's grandeur. How can it get better than that?

Chapter 18

Manitoba Geese

I couldn't pinpoint the source of the noise, but it wasn't anything I'd ever heard before while hunting. Then I realized it was my hunting partner snoring. I couldn't' blame him for dozing off, we were laying on our backs on a six inch bed of straw just as the first light of dawn crept in. We hadn't had much sleep, and it would be awhile before the first flocks of geese arrived.. and it was so comfortable there, wrapped in warm coveralls between layers of straw, in the middle of a wide Manitoba grain field. As the snoring increased I thought back to the first time I had come there to hunt geese, almost fifteen years ago. It could well have been my last trip, as poorly as things went. Thank goodness I came back.

That first year, I didn't bring anything with me but a shotgun. I didn't even own a goose decoy. I lived in Arkansas at the time, where goose hunting wasn't allowed. I had hunted Canada geese as a college student at the University of Missouri, where I was studying to become a waterfowl biologist. We would skip classes every now and then in the fall to travel to Swan Lake, an hour or so north of Columbia, where there was a federal refuge and state managed hunting around it. Hunters drew for blinds and you could rent a couple dozen decoys from the state, but the hunting wasn't much more than pass shooting. We never called, and the geese seldom decoyed. The limit was one per day, and in the first couple of hours, you could usually count on getting a shot or two at a low-flying flock, so you almost never went home empty-handed.

Out of college, I became a writer instead of a biologist, and traveled to Canada to fish on occasion. There I met a man who told me he would line me up a goose hunt with a top-notch guide from Manitoba who was anxious to get the word out to Midwesterners about the great hunting they had in his area. So in early October a friend and I traveled to Winnipeg to meet this goose-hunting guide, and when we got there he said he was unexpectedly booked up with paying hunters and didn't have time to mess with some writer he hadn't ever heard of. We had driven about 16 hours for nothing.

Since Canadian law strictly forbids the killing of bogus goose hunting guides, there was little we could do, but I wasn't going to give up and head home. An official of the Manitoba Department of Natural Resources was sympathetic to our plight, and gave me the name of a local hunter who he thought might want to help. The hunter, Swin Smith, was an experienced goose hunter, and he spent several hours showing us around, telling us how to hunt geese

Swin Smith with some homemade decoys that got us started.

and where, and then loaning us 3 dozen Canada goose decoys. They were old and bedraggled, and some were homemade, but they worked. I haven't seen him since, but he was a real gentleman and I will never forget what he did for us.

The region one hour north of Winnipeg where Smith took us is flat, fields of grain interspersed with scrubby timber Canadians call "The Bush". The southern tip of Lake Winnipeg lies to the east, and the southern tip of Lake Manitoba is to the west, and in that marshland at the foot of these two giant bodies of water, snows, blues and Canadas stage by the hundreds of thousands in mid to late September. With all the grain fields between those two marshes, that alone makes it a goose hunters paradise, but there's more. There's a place called Oak Hammock, 16 square miles of managed hunting land.... privately owned, surrounding a refuge which attracts and holds hundreds of thousands of ducks and geese. But I don't want to get too far ahead of myself, with all you readers on the edge of your seats in suspense, dying to know what happened when we tried our hand at goose hunting.

My friend Bill Gilbert was a native Arkansan who had never hunted geese, and had about halfway decided he never would after our first few hours in Manitoba. To tell the truth, neither of us figured we would have any success on our own, but Swin Smith encouraged us, and we set forth to have a try at it. The idea was to find flocks of geese feeding in fields in the evening, then ask permission to hunt there the following morning, when the flocks should return. We found the field all-right.. one with a million geese in it, or so it seemed, every kind and color. There was a farm house on the corner of the section, about a quarter mile from the geese, so with a great deal of trepidation, we set about getting permission to hunt. In Arkansas, you can get shot at by just asking permission to hunt, or perhaps be set upon by a pack of mongrel dogs raised just to deter anyone from getting as far as the back door. I just knew this

Canadian farmer would see we were from a foreign country and call the R.C.M.P to file trespassing charges against us just for getting out in his yard.

We got there before he did actually. We pulled into the drive and set there looking at that beautifully kept white farm house thinking to ourselves that there wasn't a chance in a hundred that these folks would let us dig a hole in their field and shoot their geese. We might have just turned around and left, but the farmer drove in behind us. He and his wife got out with a smile on their faces, and our confidence level rose a bit. The gentleman had on a dark suit and tie, and I told him who we were as we shook hands.

He and his wife were returning from a wedding, and Bill Richey says he remembers to this day that one of us commented on how much better Canadian farmers dressed than those from the Ozarks. All I remember is, he told us we were welcome to hunt, and then he asked us if we'd like to borrow some shovels to dig some shallow pits with. Here we were asking for permission to dig up his grain field and he was of offering to loan us shovels. And as if that wasn't enough, he said he had a bale of straw we could use to line the pit and hide beneath.

We stayed and talked to the Richeys for quite some time, then just before dark, after the geese had left, we went out and dug out a pair of pits about 6 foot long, 3 feet wide, and a foot deep. At dawn the next morning, Bill Gilbert and I were lying there looking up into the cold misty sky, absolutely convinced we didn't have a chance of luring a goose within gun range. But our borrowed decoys looked good spread around us, and there was always a chance. After all, no one ever said geese were any smarter than we were, and I felt confident that we actually had a slight edge on them in intelligence, even though we were lying under a bed of straw in a cold damp field just after first light more than a thousand miles from home..

Swin Smith had told us what I pretty much already knew about geese. Snows and blues travel in large flocks

166

as a rule, and are not easy to decoy with small spreads. Hunters who pursue them use hundreds of decoys, from the manufactured ones to diapers or plastic bags blowing in the wind. Canadas on the other hand are drawn to small sets, and decoy well in groups of two or three or 15 to 20 birds. What happened to Bill Gilbert and I that fateful morning should probably be left untold, but they say its good therapy to talk about these things.

Instead of a few geese here and a few there, all the geese in the world seemed to come in at once. There were hundreds of blues and snows, and probably a hundred or more Canadas, all coming to the spot where they had fed the previous evening, where my partner and I now waited, everything but our eyes covered with straw. There were four or five layers of geese above us, circling, funneling, dropping... talking back and forth excitedly, an experience you have to see to fully appreciate. The sight and sound of hundreds of geese in the air above you is unsettling, and Bill and I didn't know what to do.

Finally, with some of them beginning to drop in around us, I lost control and came up shooting. Well, wanting to shoot anyway. There were clumps of straw hanging to the ribbed barrel of my 3 inch magnum, and I couldn't find any beads to sight with. As the gun came up, some of the straw came back in my face. Geese are quick to react, and by the time my barrel was cleared, the easy shots were gone. I can tell you that we emptied both shotguns and shot at pretty much every goose there.

When it was all over, we had a blue goose, and two of those little dinky Canadas they call cackling geese. Bill was griping about the fact that he hadn't been able to aim at first because he had straw on his barrel

It began to rain hard shortly afterward, so we called it quits early and packed everything in, both of us thinking we had killed all 3 geese, and each therefore fairly happy with the mornings results. You have to remember we weren't expecting anything. But the best was yet to come, as Lois Richey had fixed dinner for us.

I remembered it all that day as I lay there listening to my partner snoring. Now, we never make a trip to hunt geese that we don't stop by to visit with the Richeys and have dinner with them. Occasionally we hunt on their farm or one of the neighboring farms, and we have a long list of friends in the region. Those people are the friendliest people I've ever met, and hunters from the states who behave decently will find it very easy to get permission to hunt the fields after the harvest is over. And yet, it seems that over the years there are fewer goose hunters in the area, and more geese.

After that first year, I never came back to Canada unprepared. My hunting partners and I began to acquire our own decoys, and we learned quickly how to hunt the fields. I brought a young Labrador my second year, a chocolate pup that I named Rambunctious, Ram for short. He created a different kind of problem, because as hard as it is to hide 3 hunters in a grain field, it is much harder to hide one young inquisitive 90 pound retriever. But there is one thing a powerful retriever can do easily that you probably cannot do even with a great deal of difficulty. He can chase down a crippled twelve pound Canada honker across a muddy field, or go get a snow goose that drops two hundred yards beyond the decoys. I recall too that over the years, my hunting buddies have found occasion to blame everything that goes wrong on me... Ram never did.

When Ram was young, he became a better hunting dog because of those Canada trips. There was one hunt I remember in particular in the mid-eighties when Manitoba had received heavy rain in late summer and some grain fields had little potholes of standing water. We found one field where the grain had been harvested around a small wet spot and there was a pond-sized hole of water about a foot deep with unharvested grain around it standing about three feet tall. The area was filled with mallards and pintails, and a good number of geese, and the landowner told us we could hunt it.

The following morning in early October, it was snowing and cold, with low gray skies. We threw a dozen duck decoys out on the water, placed two dozen goose decoys around the edge of the pothole and fixed a small pit on the dry ground next to it in that unharvested grain. Pintails, mallards, widgeons and gadwalls all worked that pothole all morning, and an occasional flock of geese came into our spread when we weren't shooting ducks. It was one of the greatest waterfowl hunts I've ever had. Ram was beside himself with excitement, charging after downed ducks with undying energy, and tackling the geese with growing enthusiasm. We had a limit of twelve ducks and several geese by 9:00 a.m.

My partner that trip was Mike Dodson, a long-time waterfowling companion who is somewhat competitive, a downright game-hog at times when he's hunting with me. Usually Mike has a limit before I do, partly because he's a very good shot, and because he is, after all, a game-hog! But that morning, I killed a limit of Canada geese before he

Hunters in Manitoba hunt geese from depressions dug in the middle of grain fields.

did, and Mike was beside himself. The noon shooting dead-line was drawing near, the skies were beginning to clear somewhat and Mike was one goose short. I had a long walk back to the pick-up, which I meant to retrieve and drive out onto a levee road only a hundred yards from where we had been hunting, so I left Mike there and Ram tagged along with me.

We were at the levee when I heard my hunting partner blowing his goose call, and I turned to see about six or eight Canada geese out over the field low, heading into our decoys. Three hundred yards out they were locking their wings, and zeroed in. Ram saw them too, and before I could get his attention he headed for the blind at a dead run, so he could be there to get Mike's last goose for him.

Unfortunately, the big Labrador was fast in his youth, and he arrived at Mike's side just before the geese were within range. Temptingly close, the flock flared, fought for altitude and headed for Oak Hammock's marshes to the south. I'd like to say Mike took it like a true sportsman, but lying is lying and I just can't do it. In fact, to be truthful he kicked one of the closest goose decoys a good 30 feet and even at the distance I had attained from our spread I could hear him say things that do not pertain to any type of water-fowl hunting.

Ram did better as he grew older, but Mike never has really improved much. He still kicks a decoy on occasion, and though he'll deny it, I think he's more of a game-hog than ever.

The snoring stopped abruptly. Even in his sleep Mike Dodson can hear a goose on a distant horizon. I heard them too and suddenly past memories were forgotten. We knew that in a minute or so, there would be geese dropping from the skies around us, coming in at exactly 8:00 a.m. from the big refuge lake south of us. Sometimes they are slow getting to the grain fields, but if they haven't been hunted hard they return fairly early for breakfast.

Rich Abdoler and I began calling as loud and frantically as we could, as Mike watched the long string of geese approaching on the horizon, followed by another, and yet another. Surprisingly, the first flock passed over us fairly high, but the second group didn't'. They came into the field low, passed over once out of range and came back around in a wide circle to glide in above us with their wings set. The flock of Canadas numbered about 40, and a couple out in front set down less than 20 yards from our gun barrels.

There was no straw on my barrel that morning as I raised up with a big goose right before me. He folded as I squeezed the trigger, and my partners guns were roaring on either side of me. It should have been easy to pick off a second goose as the flock fought for altitude, but I hurried and missed. My last shot was just as hurried, but I got lucky and intercepted a Canada just before it passed above me. It fell stone dead behind our pit. There were five geese on the ground around us, and another hard hit at the outer edge of the decoys.

Brandy, the young yellow Labrador on her first goose hunt, was beside herself with excitement, but she tackled the crippled goose and got the best of it. She had been lying beside me in a fairly controlled but curious manner until the shooting started. Now the young dog would be hard to get back into our shallow pit. And there was no time to waste, as there were more geese on the way. Around our field were strings of geese, approaching flocks of Canadas, and high flights of blues and snows. You never knew how long the mornings activity would last, or when a small group of live geese in a neighboring field would begin to draw incoming flocks away from you. But it seemed that our limit of five Canadas would not be long coming, and if things went well, there would be shots at some snows and blues as well.

The field where that last hunt took place was only about twelve miles from the Richeys farm where we first learned to hunt geese the right way.

I say the right way, because until I began to hunt in

171

Manitoba, most of the goose hunting I did was pass shooting, and too much of it bordered on sky-busting. To hunt geese or ducks right, there's no place for maximum range shooting. The right way is decoying waterfowl, hunting geese which are committed to your set, fooled by a spread of decoys and brought into gun range with feet extended and wings cupped.

Every fall we bag several blues and snows in Canada with a minimum of light decoys. Usually we'll set 15 or 18 snow goose decoys with a spread of perhaps three or four dozen Canada decoys, and we'll get our share of opportunities on small flocks of lightgeese. But we don't go all out for them like some hunters do. If you're after snows and blues, you need to be hunting with 80 to 120 decoys. It's not that way with Canada geese. If you are in a good field and well hidden, you can bag a limit of dark geese with 12 or 15 decoys.

In the early days, before we accumulated quantities of decoys, we did that quite often. Canada geese are intelligent birds, but not as wary as the snows.... the years of

Big foot decoys fill a grain field with lifelike spreads.

172

hunting them have convinced me of that.

Modern decoys make goose hunting today considerably easier than it was years ago. Today I use three dozen Carry-lite shell decoys that are so realistic in the field you can't imagine how they can be improved. And the shell decoys are so important because of their light weight. One hunter can carry two dozen, and that's important when you have to walk several hundred yards through soft grain fields.

Ten or twelve years ago, we actually carried floating decoys out into the fields, and I was always worn out before we got them halfway there. There'll be no more of that. In addition to the shells, which set up on stakes, we use 18 decoys that look more like geese than actual geese. They are known as Bigfoot decoys, over-sized imitations with feet that incoming flocks seem to focus on. Made by Art Ladehoff in Clinton, Iowa, Bigfoot decoys are the most expensive goose decoys, and they are large and bulky. But they are unbelievably effective. They look so much like a goose that lawn and garden centers buy them for lawn decorations, and you see them quite often sitting in a lawn owned by someone who never hunted a goose in his life. And passersby will see those geese from 60 or 70 yards away and be convinced they are live Canadas.

I don't know that you have to buy more than six or eight of them to see dramatic results. But if you could afford two dozen of them, you could hunt Canada's in the field with no other decoy's necessary, and you'd have to be a pretty poor hunter not to have success with them. Most goose hunters do as I do, and buy a few decoys each year until they have too many to hunt with anyway. When you get enough of those Bigfoot decoys you can sell all the rest. I've noticed since I began to use them, the geese will zero in on those Bigfoots no matter how many others you have or how you use them. The only problem is, they are heavier and bulkier, so I like to combine them with shell decoys when I have to walk quite a distance to hunt.

173

My hunting partner, Rich Abdoler, always brings about ten or twelve standing wind sock decoys along, and a few flying ones. I'm convinced if that's all you had you would have a problem. Rich is sold on them, and I admit that when used to complement the other decoys, they are impressive. But you need some wind for them to do their thing, and if there's no wind, don't even use them.. Last year we used three or four flying wind socks which are mounted on eight-foot poles. In the right wind, they really attract attention.

Another thing we've tried in recent years is some attachable wings called Flapperz, created by a Michigan hunter a few years back to add motion to a set of decoys. The wings, held on by velcro, make hard shell decoys look alive when the wind is right. I believe that adding some motion to a spread with the wings and wind socks is a tremendous aid to the goose hunter, but you have to know the fundamentals of creating a life-like spread with the geese you have, and you need to know something about calling geese, or at least how not to call. Most importantly, you need to know how to hide yourself, and that is an art.

We like to hunt fields of stubble where grain stalks are still scattered. Its pretty easy to use that straw-like material to line a shallow pit. We then can cover ourselves with camouflaged material and scatter the straw or grain stalks over us. If you use a retriever, you need to have a well trained dog which will lie patiently beside you, at least partially covered.

Those are things you learn by hunting geese year after year, making mistakes and achieving success as you correct them. It's easy to do in a land where there are so many geese, and the landowners so willing to allow hunting and anxious get to know the hunters from the states. In this land well to the north of Winnipeg, between the two giant bodies of water known as Lake Winnipeg and Lake Manitoba, you'll find goose hunting that will equal any you'll find anywhere. And you don't need a guide, just a basic knowledge of goose hunting and geese, the equipment to hunt them, and a good retriever not afraid to tackle a tough assignment.

It is a magnificent and unforgettable sight. The geese come with a great deal of fanfare, honking to one another, and they descend quickly by side-slipping and rolling on their backs in mid-air. Their voices reach an excited crescendo as they sweep across harvested grain fields, circling wide, then cupping their wings against the wind, rocking back and forth above the decoys with legs extended to meet the dark earth. The geese arrive in groups; as some alight, others bear in behind them, and still others circle wide. High above, a new flock is dropping with acrobatic maneuvers.

There is nothing like it, and it is spellbinding to watch. Sometimes you don't want to take the shots that present themselves, because it will end this awe-inspiring arrival of descending flocks.

One of the effective ways to hunt Canada geese in the lower Midwest is to hunt them over floating decoys on lakes and marshes. Usually, geese coming to decoys on the water are returning to a resting area after feeding in nearby fields. It's just as different the other two methods I've mentioned.. but for hunters with good boat-blinds and floating decoys, it can be great hunting. When hunting geese over water, you almost always have some duck hunting too. But in the northern grain country they are usually hunted in the fields where they feed.

To hunt geese, you need to know geese; how they behave, where they rest and how they feed. Unlike ducks, geese seldom feed in the water. They are grazers when there's no grain available, looking for green grass and vegetation on solid ground. They can walk very easily and often cover a considerable distance while grazing, or feeding across a field of grain.

Canada geese mate for life; but take a new mate if the former mate is killed. Several times I have seen a goose circle and return to the spot where its companion has fallen to a hunter's gun. But only when it was alone. I've never seen a goose leave a flock to return and search for a fallen mate, so the idea that they are so closely paired that one will not go on without it's mate seems a little far-fetched. In fact, I killed a pair of geese in Canada one fall when one returned to the decoys after the other fell. Both were females.

Canadas live much longer than most waterfowl, some surviving 15 to 20 years according to bird-banding information. And they are plentiful, increasing in number during the late '80's and 90's years by leaps and bounds. Most Canada geese, at least the bulk of the migrating flocks, nest far to the north, in a region where nesting success isn't much affected by water conditions, as ducks are in the prairie regions of southern Canada. But a late June snowstorm causes real nesting problems and occasional dips in migrating numbers.

Today, Canada geese do not migrate in the manner they did a century ago. Changing land use with widespread availability of grain in the north, have caused Canadas to stop and linger longer, and in many instances they never reach the southern states, depending on snow cover and the severity of the winter.

Of course, thousands of geese don't migrate at all. Most Midwestern states now have Canada geese in suburban areas which have grown in number to a point of being pests. These golf-course geese become semi-tame, much like flocks of geese on large reservoirs in the mid-south. On some of these lakes and in suburban residential areas as well, the geese are fed by retirees who live there and do not approve of hunting. Now there are overpopulations and overgrazing and so much goose manure in some areas you can't walk through them without slipping.

So now there are some September goose hunting seasons, and managed hunts in the outskirts of major cities like Minneapolis. And so far, nothing has really stemmed the booming numbers of these suburban flocks.

There's a great variety of Canada geese, with most biologists agreeing there are 11 subspecies. I've killed honkers up to fifteen pounds, and others only three or four pounds in weight. The former is the giant Canada, and the latter a tiny goose known as Richardson's goose. They look the same... except for size, all of the subspecies are so similar they are hard to tell apart. Most of our Canadas are lesser Canadas usually weighing from six to ten pounds, but I've heard of some giant Canadas weighing 20 pounds.

In our lower Midwestern region, most geese are killed by duck hunters who get lucky with a passing flock, but as the winter progresses and duck season ends, a few sincere goose hunters will hunt fields and waters over goose decoys.

Steel shot must be used almost everywhere, and I prefer B.B. sized shot with heavy loads for Canada geese. If they are decoying properly and your shots are at normal range, number two shot, patterned on the head and neck, is sufficient. Hunters who use the T shot and larger, are too often trying to knock down geese which are 60 yards high, and when they get one, it very often is because of a broken wing. If you are shooting at geese which are more than 50 yards out, you need to do something different.

To hunt Canada geese effectively you need to study the flocks and their movements, from resting areas on a lake or marsh to feeding areas which may be miles and miles away. When you 've figured it out, Canada goose hunting is worth the effort, and worth the wait.

Chapter 19

Sweating and Swatting

The world record for the shortest stay in a duck blind by a bonafide duck hunter occurred one September in a southern state where a teal hunter crawled into a duck blind which had become the summer home of a four-foot long water snake. The exact length of his stay was short but the height of his departure was considerable, his companions say.

He did not get a limit, but then few teal hunters care if they don't limit out in a hurry. Even so, most of us do not expect to be snake bitten while duck hunting or to become a training dummy for broods of half-grown mosquitoes on their first prowl. The dangers of duck hunting are supposed to be frostbite and hypothermia. September teal hunting, therefore is not really duck hunting, it's teal hunting . If teal were really ducks, they'd stay in Canada with the mallards and gadwalls and widgeons until October. Instead, they pick up and head south in late August as if pursued by a blue-norther blizzard.

In the early 60's, biologist s realized that teal, especially blue-wings, were only lightly harvested because of this habit of out-running the hunting season. That's when special September teal seasons were instituted. Now teal season finds me on some marshland mosquito refuge with too much camouflaged clothing and sweat dripping off my nose into my chest waders. It's almost always hotter in September than it is in midsummer, and the best place to be at such times is home on the porch, sipping iced tea and watching the ball game.

It's true that sometimes there are lots of teal and they decoy great and the shooting is fantastic, but still, four or five days of teal hunting is enough for me. And I would certainly not reccommend it to any of you. A man in a muddy marsh trying to kill a handful of biscuit sized ducks is a pitiful sight . And when you add the mosquitos, the snakes, and the 85 degree temperatures, you realize that such a man is an addict—he can't help himself.

Every year I say I'm not going to do it any more, but I always end up out there in the mud, sweating and swatting, and swearing at the last flock I missed. Looking back through the heat waves of all those Septembers, I remember the very first special season; back in 1965 if memory serves me right. I was a college freshman, always looking for a reason to go back home to the Big Piney on weekends. I couldn't remember ever seeing many blue-wings on the river in September, but I went home anyway just to give it a try.

I had an old wooden johnboat back then and used a blind attached to the bow to float the river and sneak up on and jump shoot ducks in the fall and winter. It worked very well on mallards and wood ducks in November, so I figured it would work just as well on teal in September. Of course, I took my rod and reel and fished a little. I caught a few smallmouth and goggle-eye before noon, but finally the fishing slowed down and I hadn't seen a duck.

It got fairly hot, so I stopped on a secluded gravel bar and stripped down for a swim. Lounging in the cool water, I heard the whisper of wings and looked up to see about fifteen blue-winged teal shoot past only ten or twelve yards over my head. Upstream, they veered abruptly and headed back downriver out over the timber. I thought they might come back, so I grabbed my shotgun and waded out into chest deep water at the back of my boat, prepared to give the next flock a volley of hot lead. And I was so intent on watching downstream for those teal, I wasn't even aware of the boat coming down the river from behind me.

It was two old-timers in one of my grandfathers wooden boats, slipping along and fishing quietly, with several nice bass hanging from a stringer alongside. There wasn't much I could do but stand there and let them float past.

"You ain't fishin' I don't reckon," one old man said as they drifted by.

"Teal hunting," I answered , trying to be as nonchalant as one can be while standing in mid-stream with a shotgun and no clothes on.

As luck would have it, one of the men recognized the boat. "You Fred Dablemont's grandson?" he asked. I nodded. "He know you're out here?" he asked again.

Finally I broke down and explained everything to save Grandpa's reputation around the Big Piney country and one of the old-timers allowed as how he knew I was a college boy, so he wasn't surprised to see me in such a situation.

They did say they intended to fish awhile in the next eddy just around the bend, so if I'd hurry I could go on past and maybe find that flock of teal downstream. As it turned out, I got a couple of teal that day, and might have dropped a couple more out of another flock if I hadn't been fishing again.

In the mid-seventies I began to hunt teal on some of Missouri's public waterfowl areas: Schell Osage in west-central Missouri, and Fountain Grove in north-central Missouri.

Some writer friends of mine were finding very good hunting in Kansas' Cheyenne River bottoms and along the Arkansas River in Oklahoma. Other hunters reported that teal hunting was great in eastern Arkansas as well.

By now, there were addicts in many states. As I recall, the Septembers became hotter, and mosquitos that once starved long before October's frost were going into hibernation fat on the blood of teal hunters. The sale of insect repellent skyrocketed, and duck decoys began to go on sale in August. For a time, there was some thought given to snakeproof chest waders, but I think that fizzled out.

Teal over decoys are tough to hit. They are fast and

they dodge shot patterns. Doves learned to escape hunters by watching teal. Compared to a blue-wing , a mourning dove is a tin can on a fence post.

In 1980, I hunted with another writer who actually paused at mid-morning to cut open a shotshell to see if there was any shot in it. That year we had great hunting at Schell Osage. In 1981, there were no teal at either Schell Osage nor Fountain Grove, and it was back to the Ozarks to jump shoot.

In 1982, however, conditions were just right at Fountain Grove and the marsh that had no ducks a year before was full of teal, with very few hunters. So Dave Meisner, publisher of Gun Dog , and brothers Norm and Rob Beattie drove down from Iowa, and we pitched our tents at Fountain Grove for a three-day stay. It was their first teal hunt in Missouri, and their first experience using steel shot for teal.

While today's steel shot is just as effective for waterfowl in my book, it has different speeds and patterns than lead; you have to learn how to shoot it. It wasn't as effective when ammunition companies first began to develope it. Learning to shoot steel at teal back in those days was like trying to learn to paddle a canoe in the Colorado River.

I couldn't help but smile when Dave and Norm and Rob told me about their custom of putting a quarter in a can for each missed shot, the total proceeds to finance a late-season hunting trip somewhere. It was obvious to me that these guys would soon have enough money to hunt darn near anywhere in the continental U.S. for the whole month of December.

It was quite a surprise when Meisner killed his first four teal with four shots. Rob and Norm came in owing more money than I brought with me. Our afternoon hunt showed us there were plenty of teal, and that evening in camp, we enjoyed fried teal and onions, some of the best eating I think I've ever had.

Blue-winged teal are small, but they are at the top of the list when it comes to the table. I think I'd rather eat them fried than any other way. Their diet is 75 percent vegetation with the remainder made up of insects and small aquatic life. But during late summer and fall, they feed almost entirely on vegetation, so they are very good eating when the season is on.

Most September teal hunters never realize what a beautiful bird the blue-winged drake is because they are in their late molt plumage in the fall and very drably colored.

In the spring, the blue-winged drake is an eye-catcher. Personally, I think he rivals a drake wood duck in beauty.

Blue-wings leave their southern retreats about the beginning of March, and much courtship display and competition takes place as they migrate. They take two months or more to arrive on northern breeding grounds, and when they get there, they are usually already paired up.

One April, while hunting wild turkey along southern Missouri's Big Piney River, I saw hundreds of blue-wings, apparently very content to relax on Ozark ponds and streams, because they were there for at least ten days. Floating silently along one morning listening for gobblers on the surrounding hillsides, I watched five or six teal sweep upstream and fly over in the blink of an eyelash, only a few feet above my head. Most were drakes, and I don't believe I've ever been so close to flying waterfowl. Their slate gray-bluish heads and necks looked nearly black in the early morning light, with the rump patches and half-moon behind the eye shining white as snow.

These birds do not fly as fast as hunters estimate. (A naturalist in the 1800s guessed that they fly 130 miles per hour!) Depending on the wind, their flight ranges from 45 to 55 miles per hour. They are actually not as fast in flight as larger ducks, but they have a great maneuverability, and they seem to dodge and dart in full flight.

Blue-winged teal nest in a huge triangle formed by a line from northern Nevada to the eastern Great Lakes and on to Alaska. They are not found along the East or West Coasts. The cinnamon teal, a separate but similar species, is a Westerner, seldom farther east than western Kansas.

The green-winged teal shows up during the September season occasionally, but the bulk of this species does not migrate until northern waters freeze over. I've killed green-wings over decoys in Arkansas in January, coming in with the last flights of mallards. Because it is a late migrator, it's puzzling why a few green-wings always show up with the blue-wings in September. Green-wings, like blue-wings,

184

love rivers and sand bars and mud flats. They are an ounce or so smaller than blue-wings, and their winter range is larger, extending from the West Coast to the Carolinas, Virginia, and Alabama in the east. Breeding grounds cover all of the northwestern U.S. and Canada, extending east to about the western edge of the Great Lakes.

Both species of teal found in the Central and Mississippi flyways decoy very well to mallard decoys. During that Fountain Grove trip years ago we used only fifteen to twenty decoys. The blinds were grown up in high weeds, and it was easy to get well concealed and yet still see across the marsh. Flights of teal were numerous on the second morning of our hunt, and after Meisner dropped his first blue-wing of the day with his first shot, I was a little hesitant to shoot. But he made the mistake of bragging just a little, and to the enjoyment of Norm and Rob, proceeded to miss six or seven in a row.

Huddled in the weeds watching for incoming flocks, none of us could say much about our shooting, so Dave and I bragged on our dogs instead. His female wirehaired pointer, "Max," one of the world's ugliest gun-dogs, was only a seven-month-old pup at the time, and my beautiful male yellow Labrador was just over a year old. When two or three ducks went down, it seemed both dogs wound up trying to retrieve the same bird, and the competition became fierce at times. Teal aren't as wary as most waterfowl, and hunting them is a great way to introduce a young dog to his first ducks. Both Beau and Max sat outside the blind, watched, and participated in all the action. Very often, low-flying blue-wings would pass over us only a few feet above our heads, but they came and went so swiftly that we often had no chance at a shot.

On the second day of that hunt, Rob Beattie and I were sitting on top of one of the pit blinds when a single blue-winged teal swung wide out in front of us and headed back to our decoys. I knew what it was, but I thought I'd have some fun out of Rob. "Don't shoot 'til I'm sure it isn't a wood duck," I told him. "Wait 'til I give you the word." Rob waited patiently as the duck bore in over the decoys at which point I dumped it with a single shot.

Rob was indignant. "I thought you were going to wait 'til we were sure it was a teal," he complained.

I told him I thought he knew it was a teal. "How was I suppose to know?" he said.

"That's easy Rob," I told him. "If I shoot at it, you know it's a teal!"

There were lots of pintails on the marsh that day and quite a few shovelers as well. Fountain Grove Area officials were worried about hunters confusing those two species for teal. Lone hen pintails are very easy to mistake for a blue-wing teal, and shovelers are so much like blue-wings that, unless you get a good look at the bill, you might think they are teal.

The problem is twice as bad when you are shooting into the sun or the day is dark. I used to have trouble hunting the river because young wood ducks are often mixed in with a flock of teal, and they are colored much the same in September. I was hunting with a veteran biologist once, and when a flock of shovelers swept upstream he dropped one, absolutely sure they were teal. I've made identification mistakes too, so I find little fault with someone who occasionally drops a shoveler or an immature woodie accidentally. But if you consciously attempt to make sure of the species, such mistakes will be held to a minimum.

To help make identification more positive, most states with early duck seasons open shooting hours at sunrise rather than 30 minutes before. And in a few states, a wood duck or "bonus duck" is allowed in the daily bag. It seems that during the September season, different states have much varying regulations, so don't go until you know what the shooting hours, seasons, and bag limits are in your state.

Biologists still feel that blue-winged teal are probably under-harvested... in recent years, they have done far better than other species, showing steady increases on breeding ground surveys. In 1982, the Fountain Grove Area recorded its highest harvest of blue-winged teal ever during the nine-day special season, with 2,131 bagged. The ratio of young to adult was about six and one half to one. In other words, about 86 percent of the blue-wings were immatures, an idication of an excellent hatch. But that's not surprising. These little ducks sometimes hatch from 12 to 15 eggs.

Biologists easily determine immature teal by looking at the tail feathers. In an immature teal, there's a notch in the end of the tail feathers, while the tail feathers of an adult bird are pointed.

Of course, you never know where the teal will be until September when water conditions and the weather dictate the hunting, but when the temperature drops below 50 degrces a few nights in a row, blue-wings will be on the move. My duck-hunting buddies will be out there each year in September, new meat for a million marshland mosquitoes. The mosquitoes almost always have a good hatch!

Chapter 20

Letters from a Duck Hunter

SEPTEMBER 15, 1986
Dear Joe,

Got your letter yesterday, and I was afraid you were thinking along those lines. I sure hate to hear you and your son won't be coming down this fall to hunt. Him and my boy has gotten to be awful good friends over the years and I know they was both lookin' forward to another hunt. How old was they when we first took the two of 'em out duck huntin'.....only 7 or 8 if I remember right. Then I remember the year we decided they was old enough to shoot a few ducks and we gave both of 'em those little Winchester 20 gauge single shots. That's a day that'll live forever in my mind. It's the most shotgun hulls I ever seen in a duck blind and the fewest ducks. But I don't know that either of us shot much better when we was 10.

Now look at those boys...dang near growed men, not long from the time they'll be goin' out on their own. If you think about it Joe, we could be takin' grandsons out duck hunting in another 15 years or so.

Course that don't seem like such a long time now....not like it did when we was first huntin' together with our dads. What was that, near onto 30 years back if I ain't miscalculatin'.

Dang it Joe, I never thought it would come to this, us not havin' enough ducks to hunt, to make it worth the goin'. I can't hardly believe they're cuttin' back to 2 mallards.

I reckon though if I had to drive that far I'd give some thought to not comin' either. Course I'll go anyway, even if they just allowed 1 mallard. I got this old Lab to think of.

He wants to get out there and get him a duck or two to retrieve, and I expect a pair of mallards will be enough for the old rascal. Sorta hoped I could get that young dog started this year. An then, I can't imagine not takin' my boy out on openin' week-end even if they ain't many ducks. It means more to him than about anything else we do, and I don't think he cares much if he kills a whole sackful....4 mallards between the two of us won't be so bad.

Thinkin' back on it Joe, we didn't kill many ducks when we was boys. Remember there for awhile you could only kill one wood duck. If it wasn't for all them old pictures, I wouldn't remember how many ducks we ever got.

But I still laugh when I think about that time we shot them coots and our dads made us clean 'em and eat 'em. And remember when you fell in that time and your dad jumped in and pulled you out. Boy that was scary. I remember building up that big fire and drying out clothes most of the morning. We thought our dads were just about the bravest and strongest men in the world.

Now that I think about it Joe, it wasn't the ducks we killed that made those trips so great. We were lucky boys to have dads like that.....they never give too much thought to all the things they had to do...come Saturday morning we all hunted ducks. What I remember is those old dogs snorin' in the corner and the hot chocolate and the home-made donuts and the cold baloney and cheese sandwiches. And those danged hip waders that were always too big for me.

Remember that time when your dad and my dad got into the argument over who killed that snow goose, and didn't speak to each other for two hours. Then they finally got to feelin' bad about the example they were settin' for us boys and shook hands and apologized to each other, and then had another big argument, each one insistin' the other ought to have the goose.

Yeah Joe, we were lucky boys. Wish we could have another day in the blind with the two of 'em, even if we didn't see a doggone duck.

I expect our boys will say that someday. I expect they won't remember what the limit's were, or how many they shot. I hope they get to see a few ducks in 20 or 30 years, what with the way we're losing our wetlands. That's one reason I'll go ahead and buy a duck stamp this year, even if there ain't many ducks. And I'm gonna go to that Ducks Unlimited banquet over at Prairieville in October. I can't afford to bid on none of that stuff they auction off, but I always get a good meal and I can spare the 25 bucks. Maybe someday it'll all pay-off and we'll have ducks come back thick as flies. Heck Joe, even if they don't, we gotta keep tryin'.

Well my boy's gonna be disappointed when I tell him you ain't gonna make it this year, but maybe next year. I hope you don't wind up havin' to come by yourself in the future. These boys are liable to start gettin' more interested in girls than they are in ducks.

We'll think about you while we're out there. It just ain't gonna be the same.

Sam

OCTOBER 1, 1986
Dear Joe,

Well I've got to tell you, your letter comes as a surprise. I'm sure tickled you've changed your mind. My boy's just beside hisself with excitement, and the wife is planning a big week-end. She said she'd make you some of those rubarb pies you like so well, and she said to tell your wife while we're huntin' the two of 'em will go over to Prairieville and go shoppin' at that new mall. See you in November.

Sam

P.S. I can't help but wonder...what made you change your mind.

November 1997
Dear Joe,

Well, we opened the season yesterday, and I guess there'll never be another opener like it around here. The first week-end in November and we had a snow like it was Christmas. It got cold last week, and it has been getting down into the low 30's at night, but we didn't expect a snow. You remember Dave Brewster from down the road.... never been on a duck hunt in his whole life 'til yesterday. Well, he wanted to see what it was like so he bought all his stamps and a box of steel shot and I loaned him my old automatic. We headed up to the Brushy Creek arm of the lake and I noticed it was spitting snow just a little when we left, temperature about 30 I'd guess. We met my long-time duck-huntin' buddy, Al Norflinger, there at the ramp, and by that time it had turned into a veritable blizzard ... wind out of the north, flakes as big as goose feathers, still just a little under freezing. Well we knew it wasn't going to stick, but how the devil are you going to motor up to the marsh, 2 or 3 miles away, when its pitch black and the snow is so heavy you can't see the front of the boat from the front of the boat.

Things were complicated by the fact that Al went and got himself a young Labrador from some half-fast dog breeder over by Murphey's slough and his dog and my pup decide they don't like each other. So there we were trying to put on chest waders and load decoys and break up a dog fight. Then we are in the boat ten minutes later trying to keep from getting lost in the snowstorm and these two young dogs are trying to assert which of the two should get the best seat, so we have to stop and break up another dog-fight.

We never did get where I wanted to hunt, but Al said he recognized wherever it was we wound up. I don't think he did.. .I believe he was as lost as I was but it was getting right on to shooting hours so I gave in and we set out about 3 dozen decoys. I know ol' Dave Brewster was wishing he had never mentioned an interest in duck hunting. I figure he doubted he'd ever see his family again when we left that boat ramp and lost all points of reckoning, all of us just try- ing to keep the snow out of our eyes and nose. But by golly he was enjoying it just at first light, because there were ducks everywhere! We were trying to get the blind situated on my boat, and there were mallards dropping down out of the snow all around us.

Fifteen minutes after shooting hours you still could- n't see very well because of the heavy snow, but we got the shotguns loaded, blew the duck calls a few times and watched about 15 mallards circle once, in and out of the white haze right over us, and then drop in on top of us. Al and I let 'em have it, and both of us dropped 2..., or I got 3 and he got 1, I ain't sure which. Anyway I'm wondering why ol' Dave hasn't shot yet, with mallards all over us, and I'll be darned if he didn't get his scarf caught in the mecha- nism of my old automatic, and he still hasn't got it closed yet. So I'm trying to help him get his scarf out of the breach, and Al is out trying to get his pup, Dufus, to bring in a duck. My dog, Magnum, goes out on his own and gets the first drake he can find, and about that time Al's pup decides that's the one he wants. Four drake mallards on the water and these two Labradors are into it over which one gets the first one! Good thing the water was shallow or they'd have drowned Al.

Finally we kind of got things calmed down and had another go at a new flock of ducks, and in 30 minutes we had a limit. I ain't never seen anything like it on opening day. Flights of green-winged teal buzzin' us every now and then, mallards dropping in like they had come all the way from Manitoba overnight, one bunch of widgeons and gad-

walls and even some divers of one sort or another. And two good dogfights in the middle of it all.

Magnum worked well and actually old Dufus didn't do half-bad..., they didn't get all the ducks, but Al and I helped with the ones they couldn't find. I told him if he was going to go out and get him a dog he could have come to me and got a pup free, and a good one at that. I bet he paid 50 dollars for that dog, and even at that it wasn't no bargain.

Anyway we like to never found that boat ramp, but the snow quit about 9 and before noon the sun was shining, not a patch of snow anywhere. That was yesterday. Didn't do much good this morning after the front passed. The wind didn't blow, it was clear and warm and the ducks didn't fly. Even the dogs got along. Wish you could have been here yesterday though, it was just like old times.

March, 1998
Dear Joe,

I'm sure you remember old Ed Bradbury and Maggie, you haven't been gone that long. Years ago we ducks on the slough over on the back of Ed's farm, where you got to floundering around in the mud and nearly got in over your hip boots.. Well, Ed was in the pool hall last Saturday most of the afternoon and returned home to find Maggie lying dead on the living room couch. If you don't remember Ed, I'm sure you remember Maggie. In her younger days there wasn't a man in these parts who didn't envy old Ed. Everyone use to wonder how in the dickens he wound up with her. Anyway, she's gone! Doc Harris told Preacher Bishop this morning that he figured it was her heart but no one will ever know. Ed is taking it pretty hard, but that's to be expected, as close as they were.

I talked to him just last week at the drugstore when he was in getting her some medicine and he said at the time she just didn't feel like getting out of the pick-up. That's not at all like Maggie, you know how outgoing she was. I spoke

195

to her that evening but she didn't pay much attention, she was just sitting there looking out the window as if she didn't even know who I was. I didn't realize how old she was getting, but if you think about it, Ed brought her to this country nigh onto 15 years ago. I remember she didn't like it at first, and Ed thought about taking her back to the city, but Maggie was quick to make friends and in no time at all it was like she'd been here all her life.

The two of them were inseparable, every Saturday when Ed came in town to buy feed, she'd ride along, sitting right over next to him as if she were afraid he was going to get away from her. They'd drop by the filling station on the way home and he'd buy her an ice cream while he had a bottle of pop. Of course she was a golden-haired beauty back then, back before she put on so much weight. I'm sure that getting so heavy was hard on her health, but Maggie just loved to eat, and Ed bought her anything she wanted.

They had her funeral on Sunday afternoon, but not too many of Ed's friends were there and I guess Ed's pretty upset about that too. But shucks it was all so fast most of them were gone or didn't know about it until Monday or Tuesday. I'd have been there if I hadn't been hunting ducks. I thought the world of her. In fact I never told anyone this, but she came over to my place once when Ed made that trip to the city and spent most of the day. We went for a swim down at the creek. But she was a smart one... she was back home an hour before Ed was. She was partial to me and one of Ed's neighbors, old Horace Glitch. She'd get a little peeved cause she couldn't go in the pool hall with Ed, and she'd sneak off down to the river where Horace was bank-fishing and drinking beer, and not come in til after dark. Ed never did know where she'd been, and still don't I reckon. That Maggie loved beer even more than ice cream.

Some of his friends think it's ridiculous for Ed to be carrying on this way, but I understand how much he thought of Maggie. And Ed doesn't have anyone else, his wife left him 8 or 10 years ago. She told him to choose between them and he chose Maggie. Who could blame him, that wife of his never shut up, and she spent money like it grew on trees. And she constantly found fault with old Ed. Maggie never did... anything Ed did was all-right with her. And if he told her to go get something for him, she went, with never a whimper nor a hesitation. Well to all those who say it's silly for a man that age to grieve so over a dog, I say they don't know what it's like to lose a good Labrador! That Maggie was a sweetheart.

Well, I'd best sign off Joe. I want to take a couple of these young Labs out in the morning and see if we can work some ducks. We had the first hard freeze two weeks ago and a skiff of snow last night. The mallards and the green-wings are in pretty good, and the wood ducks are long gone. Hope you can get down soon.. the dogs all miss you.

Sam

Chapter 21

Gronk and the Beginnings

It was late fall in the year of...well it was long ago, during a period of time when years were not really kept track of... when stories were related to future generations by pictures painted on rock cave walls, and men planned only for the coming day around a crackling campfire which had cooked the accomplishments of the previous one. And there, back then, is when it all began, with a woodland bluff-dweller native American named Gronk.

Actually his name was something else in the language of the day, but since it was an unwritten language and no one could understand it if we used it, we will translate the names and everything which was said that night, into English.

The women and children of that ancient tribe along a tributary of the lower Mississippi river had long retreated to the warmth of nearby huts and caves, where they slept rolled in skins of elk and deer and buffalo. Several men rested around the fire, listening to Gronk complain about having to eat too much elk, deer and buffalo.

"I tell ya, I'm just tired of gnawing burnt meat off the bone and making clothes out of their hides," he said, "it's time to try ducks."

"I gotta admit those ducks are awful good to eat," chipped in one of the older men, a fellow by the name of Skrog. "But you'd have to get a bunch of them to feed everyone, and you can't hardly get close to 'em."

Gronk's eyes brightened, though you could hardly tell it, there in the darkness. "Aha," he said, "that's where my plan comes in."

One of the men sitting closest to the fire let out a groan.

"Here we go again with those fake ducks of his... .Gronk sits around cutting fake ducks out of dead limbs and thinks he's going to trick ducks to fly in and set down beside 'em so he can shoot em."

There was a spattering of laughter around the fire, and Gronk was indignant, though you couldn't see it so much with just the campfire for light. His fake ducks looked really good, and he had tried them on the river with some promising results, though they were bad to float off in the current.

A real smart-aleck of the tribe, known as Zvork, ridiculed the idea."Heck Gronk, if we carved a fake woman out of a piece of wood, and set her up out in the woods somewhere, would you run up to join her for dinner."

Gronk was unperturbed. "I tell you I've seen it work," he said, "a dozen or more of those ducks flew over and I made a quacking sound and they landed right in my artificials."

Suddenly the laughter was uncontained. Another of the older men, a fellow by the name of Lornf, was slapping his knee and hee-hawing. "You made a quacking sound?" he roared. "You made a quacking sound? Can you fellers see that picture? Old Gronk out there up to his halfway in the reeds, hiding from those ducks and making quacking sounds..."

By now, two or three of the elders were rolling around on the ground holding their sides, while Gronk grew madder and madder. Of course you couldn't see that, there in the darkness, because as a general rule that particular tribe had an angry look about them anyway. But Gronk was really peeved and he yelled out that everyone could laugh all they wanted, but he had dropped 4 or 5 of the big green-headed ones and had et them all by hisself and meant to make pillows out of the feathers.

The laughter subsided a bit then. Not many families of the woodland tribe had pillows back then and when you started talking about duck-feather bedding you got some

200

attention. "You're making that up," Skrog said, "last time you tried them fake ducks they all kept floating down the river on you."

"I solved that problem," Gronk said with a smug look on his face which was fairly hard to see in the flickering firelight. "I tied leather thongs around their necks with a rock at the other end... .now they just set there and bob around like real ducks. And the quacking works too by gork," (gork being a term of profanity in that time). "Lornf wouldn't laugh if he could imitate ducks well enough to bring something to a meal besides his big belly."

At that, Lornf, something of a hothead in his younger days, jumped to his feet with his bow and arrow and fired a wild shot over Gronk's head. As he was restrained, the well-respected tribal elder, Harvey, jumped to his feet. "Bosh-rang you Lornf, you farl-maggled gridgen," (more profanity... Harvey was a bad one to cuss) "you'll wake up the women with that shooting!"

As tempers cooled, one of the younger men spoke up. "Maybe we shouldn't be so quick to discard this idea," he said, "after all there are only a few hundred deer and elk and buffalo and at times there are a million of those ducks."

"And they are fine eating," Zvork chipped in, "except for the ones that eat fish."

"That's understandable," Skrog said, "I remember once a few years back when the huntin' was poor and I ate fish for 2 or 3 weeks...my old lady wouldn't hardly let me in the cave."

"The eating part of it aside," reflected Harvey, "there's something to be said for pillows... feather pillows for everybody."

"Maybe we could come up with enough for a whole bed," came a voice from the far corner of the fire.

"It's settled then," Harvey said, "we'll give Gronk's fake ducks a chance. We'll fix us up some hiding places down along the river.. everybody with plenty of arrows.. .and we'll let Gronk do the quacking. When we get a bunch of 'em in, we'll have roast duck and pillows."

"It sounds good," Skrog said with some reservation in his voice, "but there's another problem... .who's going to swim out in that freezing water and chase down the dead and wounded ducks?"

There was complete quiet.... no one had thought about that. You couldn't eat and make pillows out of a bunch of dead ducks you couldn't get. And besides that, back in those days, swimming hadn't been perfected yet.

They all remembered a tribe member named Plunk who had managed to swim across the river during the summer and was still living alone on the other side because he couldn't get up the nerve to try it again the other direction.

Everyone contemplated the problem and how to solve it, and for awhile there was silence except for Lornf's stomach growling.

And then Gronk cleared his throat. "Well," he said timidly, "I have given that some thought." His comrades sat quietly waiting to hear his plan. Gronk had gone from something of a laughing stock to a man of credibility.

"You remember... during that famine we had some time back most of you ate your dogs," Gronk continued, "and most of you couldn't understand why I didn't... well I've been working with that dog, and I think I can teach him to go out and bring back the ducks we get!"

For just a moment, it was quiet, and then somebody snickered and somebody else laughed. In a matter of seconds, it had grown to loud guffawing, and there was again knee-slapping and rolling on the ground. Somebody screamed above the laughter, "He's gonna teach his dog... .aaa ha ha har har hah hoo. . . .he's gonna teach his dog to swim out and get ducks...."

In the uproar, no one noticed that Gronk had taken all he could endure. Made insane by the laughter, he picked up a burning branch from the fire and swung it at the smart-aleck Zvork. In seconds a free-for-all had broken out, and there was chaos and bedlam around the fire.

Back in the cave, Gronk's dog, Treever, slept next to the buffalo hide where the feather pillow was hidden, dreaming of ducks on the water, and his master's praise as he swam out to retrieve each and every one. Somehow he sensed that from that day forward, he and his descendants would finally be secure.

And while it is true that some pointing dogs were eaten on occasion in years to come, good retrievers have been treasured and protected even during years of famine, except for a few isolated cases in Arkansas and Louisiana. As for Gronk, history says little more about him, although according to a story on a cave wall, he was trying desperately during his later years to make a pair of chest waders out of beaver skins.

If you aren't much of a duck hunter, you can always write poetry.

Chapter 22

Poetry for the Duck Hunter

I have noticed that poetry was very popular with outdoorsmen at the beginning of the century. Some of those old magazines from that era carried quite a bit of it. You won't see that much nowadays. I figure that if you can sell poetry to an outdoorsman in this day and time, you have accomplished something comparable to selling a poodle dog to a market hunter.

However, few of us poets are out for money or acclaim. Take Elizabeth Bartlett Browning or Robert Louis Sandburg, who actually made very little money. Not trying to change the subject, but have you ever noticed how famous poets had really long names. If you'll remember, when you were a kid in school no literature teacher ever had you reading poetry by a Bob Smith or Bill Jones. Everyone who wrote poetry had long names with a middle name in there to make it sound more impressive. That's one reason why I believe I could have made it big if folks hadn't got sick of poetry just about the time I was born. My name is as long as anyone's, especially if you use the original French spelling. Larry Arthur Dableaumonte' contains almost as many letters as that Browning woman's name. And half the time her poetry never rhymed, while I never once wrote a poem that didn't rhyme. To tell the truth, lots of that poetry we had to read in junior high school never made a lick of sense either, and as I remember it we had to spend all our time trying to figure out some hidden meaning from something you couldn't make heads nor tails of. Well, no one can say my poetry doesn't make just as much sense as anything else I write!

You may well be asking yourself what all this has to do

with waterfowl hunting or retrieving dogs, if you have gotten this far. Just bear with me. Many years ago I got the idea of poetry for the waterfowler.. .poems which really rhyme and are so simple that any duck hunter can understand them, even the ones I hunt with. Poems published in a little waterproof paperback so that a hunter can take it into the marsh with him, and pull it out during slack periods to get a little inspiration, or soothe his frayed nerves after tearing a hole in his best waders. You can probably think of a hundred different times you would have enjoyed sitting back and reading some duck-hunting poetry in a remote duck blind, just you and your dog with a hot cup of soup.

I originally thought of entitling this book."Poetry for the Duck Hunter". But it would have taken too long to write it. But no book on duck-hunting could be complete without some poems, so here's the best I could come up with.... each and every poem so simple and easy to understand no literature teacher would ever strain to find any hidden meaning, and best of all, each and every poem rhymes.

This first one was inspired by something that actually happened to me. For that matter, so are all the rest of them. At this point, I have entitled the first one... "Poem Number 1", which might give you some insight into the title of the second one. If you're sitting back in your favorite easy chair with your pipe lit and your old Labrador sleeping by the fireside, then here goes;

Poem Number 1

In the darkness just before the dawn, we're ready for the hunt.

The boat is in the water, filled with everything we'd want.

There's a norther headed southward, and the ducks are down, they say.

There's little time to waste, because, the blind's two miles away.

The Labrador is in the boat, three dozen decoys sacked.

We've extra duck calls stored away, hot thermos bottles packed.

The lunch box—overfilled again, with baloney, cheese and crackers.

A feller gets plumb hungry, when he's out there huntin' quackers.

We've got pump guns in their cases, got the 10-horse on the boat.

Heavy socks and gloves and waders, and a goose-down huntin' coat.

Shells.. .we 've got aplenty, two's and fours—steel shot.

So crank that dad-blamed motor, or is there something we forgot?

You can hear the ducks aflyin'... daylights comin" fast.

Yeah, we brought some of dang near everything, but not one ounce of gas!

Well you can understand why we wouldn't publish the very best of the poems first. But you'll like this next one if you are old enough to remember the point system, back when hen mallards were worth 70 points and drakes worth 25, and when you reached 100 you had a limit. Then there were some 10 point ducks which allowed you to do more shooting, and some 100 point ducks too, which very often ended the hunt after just one shot. The 100 pointers were the redheads and canvasbacks. This next poem, known as "Poem Number 2", is based on that old point system, and the kind of luck I've had since I was born.

207

Poem Number 2

Shootin' hours are on us, there's two ducks across the spread

One flys off unblasted, and the other falls stone dead.

Ol' Blackie's gone to get 'im, best retriever there could be.

By the time my buddies get a duck, I may have two or three.

Them Federal boys, they done all-right. This point system, it's O.K.

Shoot pintail, teal and widgeon, and you can hunt all day.

All in all, it suits me fine, but there's one place where they blundered.

A greenheads only twenty-five points, but a canvasbacks a hunderd.

Yeah, shootin' hours is just begun, there's mallards streakin' south,

And here comes ol' Blackie proud as punch, with my limit in his mouth.

So I'll take my canvasback and go, but I've got an awful hunch,

If it'd been a flock of mallards, I'd a missed the whole dang bunch.

This last poem may be the best of the bunch because it deals with a modern day phenomenon known as a Ducks Unlimited Banquet. Frankly I have been to several, and nothing ever made me feel any poorer. I couldn't afford to bid on some of the door prizes! And I never have partaken of alcoholic beverages, partly because of that same reason.

A glass of tea will only run about 50 cents, and I've seen some of my cousins spend enough on a few drinks to buy most of the tea and coffee I'll drink til after the first of the year. But they say the alcohol loosens you up a little bit, to help you have a good time and not worry about spending a little money for the good cause of buying habitat for the ducks. One night, two of my cousins got so loosened up they decided to get on opposite sides of the room whereupon each would bid on the shotgun so they'd be sure one of them got it.. This poem isn't so much about what happens at the banquet, it's an account of a very traumatic encounter one of my friends had as he returned home from one. I call this one "The Banquet"

The Banquet

The D.U. Banquet was held last week, and my wife
    warned me in advance,

That if I bought any guns, or came home drunk, I'd be
    taking an awful big chance.

Remembering my spouse's wise advice,

I only drank a few.

But due to a flat and a bridge washed out,

I got home sometime after two.

I parked the car in the neighbors lawn, just to keep from
    disturbing my wife,

But awaiting me in the darkness,

was a struggle for my very life

For there on the lawn in the moonlight, sat a beast with a
    horrible face.

And I knew in a minute that thing in the grass was a creature from outer space.

It sat low on the ground with four short legs, it's torso was solid and square,

With a little round head and a long shiny tail, that stuck straight up in the air.

My only thought was my wife and kids,

as the blood flowed hot in my veins.

With a snarl on my lips and fire in my heart, I became a murderous fiend.

I dealt a chop to the base of the skull. A hard knee and a cross body press,

But it met my attack with a defense superb, And I lay at it's feet in the grass.

With a will to live that was stronger than death, I rose to continue the fight.

The stone-age man was awakened in me,

As we traded fierce blows in the night.

And just as I seemed at the end of my strength, as I stood at the brink of defeat

One last crashing blow from my lightning right fist, brought the thing to it's end at my feet

I staggered wearily into the house, and collapsed in a heap on the bed.

And when I awakened the following morn,

I looked up at my wife and I said,

"Thank heavens you're safe dear, and how are the kids?" She replied that they too were all-right.

So then I poured forth the shocking details of my clash

with the beast in the night.

My wife looked at me with suspicion and said, Your
  story's the truth, I can tell.

For there are signs of a struggle outside on the lawn,

And the mower is torn all to hell.

Well I guess that's a good one to end on, sort of an
Edgar Allen Poe type of poem. Most of the rest of them aren't
as grim as that one was.

If I had more room I'd get into some of my romantic
stuff, like, Violets are blue and roses are red, women who
love duck hunters are pretty darn desperate! I guess I need
to find a color that rhymes with "desperate". And I've been
having some trouble with one in particular that someone
might help me with. It start's out "There was a young duck
hunter from Minneapolis."

Other books by Larry Dablemont

Ain't No Such Animal

Greatest Wild Gobblers
Lessons Learned from Old Timers and Old Toms

The Front Bench Regulars
Wit and Wisdom from Back Home in the Hilla

Rivers to Run
How to Float & Enjoy the Streams of the Midwest

An Old Fashioned Fisherman
Angling Experiences and Adventures

Dogs, Ducks and Hat-Rack Bucks
Short Stories for the Outdoorsman

Ridge Runner
From the Big Piney to the Battle of the Bulge

**Lightnin'
Ridge Books**
Box 22
Bolivar • MO 65613

Author Larry Dablemont is an Outdoor Writer-Photographer from southern Missouri who has been hunting ducks since boyhood. With a degree in wildlife management from the University of Missouri, Dablemont once dreamed of being a waterfowl biologist. A full-time writer and photographer since 1970, he has published hundreds of articles about waterfowl hunting for newspapers and magazines such as Peterson's Hunting, Outdoor Life, Field and Stream and Gun Dog, to name a few. He currently writes a weekly column for 35 newspapers in Missouri, Arkansas and Kansas, and is working on publishing a series of outdoor books. He also raises a limited number of old-style, hunting Labradors and Lab puppies.